Success.
guides

Standard Grade
Computing Studies

Richard Ellis

Contents

Introduction

Unit 1 – Computer applications

Unit 2 – Communications and networks

Unit 3 – Industrial and commercial applications

Unit 4 – Computer systems

Unit 5 – The exam and assessment

Unit 6 – Exam-style questions and answers

Unit 7

Studying and preparation

Using this book

This book has been carefully prepared to cover the Standard Grade Computing Studies course in a concise form so that it is more manageable than a full-scale textbook. Leaving aside the question pages, the course notes only come to about fifty pages — which can be easily learned with a bit of effort. If you absorb all the information in this book then you will be in a very good position to tackle the exam at all levels.

Some students can simply read over this book to absorb the information while others might find it more helpful to write out sections of text as a memory aid.

You might find it helpful to highlight important or difficult blocks of text. Obviously don't do this if the book belongs to your school!

Glossary

The glossary at the end of this book extends to several pages. This is because in computing there are a lot of definitions and acronyms that are often asked for in the exam. If you can learn the glossary well then you can pick up a lot of easy marks in the exam. Give the book to a friend or relative and get them to ask you terms from the glossary.

Other resources

There are several other written materials available for Standard Grade Computing. These materials are useful but the best way to target the exam in a focussed way is to learn the material in this book, which is designed entirely to prepare you for the exam. Full-scale textbooks are an excellent resource to gain wider information but sometimes it can be hard to sift out the exact details that you need to know.

Study area

It might seem obvious but try to find an area to study in which is well-lit, comfortable, quiet and neither too hot or too cold. If you feel relaxed you will concentrate better and remember more.

Cramming

Studies have shown that cramming is not an efficient way of studying for exams.

You will remember much more if you study in lots of small doses over a long period of time rather than in a few intense periods of study just before the exam. If you leave things to the last minute then you will underachieve in the exam.

Avoid stress

People have different natures and some people become more stressed about exams than others. If you are inclined to stress over exams you can make things better by taking plenty of exercise and making sure that you get enough sleep. Avoiding stressful people is probably a good idea at exam time.

One last thought

Before you read the rest of this book, remember that it is actually a very pleasant experience to sit an exam when you have prepared yourself. If you can learn the contents of this book you will be surprised by the feeling of confidence that gives you — because the exam is not difficult when you know your subject.

General purpose packages 1

Hardware and software

Hardware refers to the physical parts of a computer such as the mouse, floppy disc drive and processor chip.

Software refers to the programs that the computer can run such as word processing, graphics, databases and the operating system.

General purpose packages

General purpose packages are programs that can be used for lots of different tasks.

For example a word processing program could be used to write a letter, make a poster or produce a newsletter.

Word processing, databases, spreadsheets and graphics are examples of general purpose packages.

Files can be saved in standard file formats so that the data they contain will be recognised by other computer programs. This makes it easier to transfer data between different programs.

Standard file formats exist for different types of data such as text, sound, graphics and video.

Some examples of standard file formats for these data types are given below:

text: ASCII, RTF; **sound:** MP3, WAV;
graphics: JPEG, GIF; **video:** real, MP4.

CREDIT

Top Tip
Learn the examples of standard file formats for each data type.

Human Computer Interface

The human computer interface (HCI) is a term to describe the way in which the user communicates with a program.

Most modern programs use a WIMP (Windows Icons Menus Pointer) HCI in which the user interacts with the program using a pointing device such as a mouse. A WIMP interface uses graphics and so is also known as a GUI (Graphical User Interface).guide to a program. This is useful to get an idea of the main features of a software package.

WIMP

A WIMP interface is user friendly because the user can simply use a pointer to select options on pull-down menus and click on icons that represent tasks. This means that a non-expert user can quickly learn how to use a new program without having to learn a lot of complicated commands.

Toolbars

A toolbar is a collection of related icons. For example a drawing toolbar could have icons for a pen, a rubber and a fill colour.

Keyboard shortcuts

Expert users can find a WIMP HCI slow and clumsy. Many software packages provide keyboard shortcuts so that an expert user can quickly hit a combination of keys on the keyboard to do the same function as a pull-down menu option.

Customizing the HCI

The interface can be altered to suit the individual user.

Changes can be made to the icons, the font sizes and colours used in windows and menus and the sounds made when actions (such as emptying the wastebasket) are performed.

Making things easier

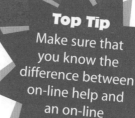

Top Tip
Make sure that you know the difference between on-line help and an on-line tutorial.

On-line help is help available within a program on how to do a specific task.

This can be preferable to using a manual as it can be searched quickly with keywords.

An on-line tutorial is a step-by-step lesson that gives an overall guide to a program. This is used to get an idea of the main features of a software package.

A wizard is a dialogue between the user and the program, guiding the user through a task. An example would be a wizard to guide you through the installation of a program.

Templates are documents that have a layout and structure already in place that can be used as a basis for other documents. This saves the user time since he/she does not need to start from a blank document.

Quick Test

1. Is a database an item of hardware or software?
2. If a user was stuck on a specific feature of a program, would he/she use the on-line help or the on-line tutorial?
3. Which general purpose package would you use to store information on 200 celebrities?
4. What is a JPEG?

Answers 1. Software 2. On-line tutorial 3. A database 4. A standard file format for graphics

General purpose packages 2

Accuracy and security

Accuracy

It is essential that data entered into a computer is accurate, i.e. it is correct and free from errors.

For example, it is extremely important that data entered to control the flight of a space craft is accurate.

Security

Often it is important that data held on a computer is kept secure. This means that it is kept private and confidential. This can be achieved with the use of passwords to control access to data and physical security to control access to computers – they can be put in locked rooms and locks can be put on their keyboards.

For example, it is important that patients' medical records are kept secure.

Dynamic and static links

CREDIT

Data can be linked between two documents. For example, data in a spreadsheet can be linked to data in a graph.

The link can be either static or dynamic.

Static link

Changes to the data in the source document WILL NOT result in changes to the data in the other document.

Dynamic link

This is a live link so that changes to the data in the source document WILL result in changes to the data in the other document.

Top Tip
Know the difference between a static link and a dynamic link.

Integrated packages

An integrated package is a program that has two or more general purpose packages. Most integrated packages have word processing, spreadsheet, database and graphic elements.

Integrated packages have both advantages and disadvantages over individual programs.

Advantages
There is a common HCI so that it is easier to learn all the different programs.
It is easy to transfer data between the different sections.
Links can be set up between the different programs.

Disadvantages

The programs in an integrated package are often less powerful and have fewer features than individual dedicated programs.

Legislation

CREDIT

There are several laws concerned with computing. In this course you need to know about three of them.

Data Protection Act

This act is concerned with the rights of individuals who have their personal details held on computer databases. The organisations that hold such details include the government, the police, banks, supermarkets, medical practices and colleges. These organisations have to comply with the requirements of the Data Protection Act.

The data subject is the person whose data is being held.

The data users are the people in the organisation who use the data.

The requirements of the act include:

- the organisation holding the data must register with the data protection registrar;
- the data subject has a right to see what data is held about him/ her;
- mistakes in the data must be amended;
- the data must be made secure;
- Data that is no longer required should be deleted.

Computer Misuse Act

This act makes malicious activities, such as hacking and sending viruses, illegal.

Copyright, Design and Patents Act

This act makes it illegal to make copies of items such as software, music and literature without the permission of the people who produced these items.

Quick Test

1. State two ways of making data held on a computer secure.

2. What is an integrated package?

3. In a medical centre the patients' data is held on computer. Who are the data users in this situation?

4. Which computing law covers the sending of viruses?

Answers 1. Use passwords or physical security such as locks on doors or keyboards 2. A software package consisting of two or more general purpose packages 3. The doctors, nurses and secretaries 4. The Computer Misuse Act

Test your progress

Questions

1. Is a computer keyboard an item of hardware or software?

2. What does the acronym WIMP stand for?

3. Why are documents sometimes saved in a standard file format?

4. Name two standard file formats used for graphics.

5. What name is given to a group of related icons?

6. Which computing law covers the copying of music files?

7. How can templates save users time when creating documents?

8. What is the name of a program which gives users lessons on how to use a software package?

9. Give an advantage of using on-line help instead of a manual.

10. How can data stored on a computer be kept secure?

11. What is meant by 'data must be accurate'?

12. Sophie changes the numbers in a spreadsheet and a graph which is linked to the spreadsheet data automatically changes. What type of link is this?

13. What is meant by a static link between two documents?

14. Name two types of general purpose package that you would expect to find in an integrated package.

15. Why is an integrated package easier to learn than separate individual packages?

16. Which computing law is concerned with hacking into confidential data?

17. What is a data subject?

18. Wendy has poor eyesight and finds it difficult to read the information in pull down menus and dialogues boxes on her computer.
    How can Wendy alter her computer to make it easier for her to use?

19. John is unhappy that the data stored by his employer has errors about the number of days that he has been off sick in the past year.
    How can John make use of a legal act to correct this situation?

20. Integrated packages are cheaper than buying individual general purpose packages and provide a common HCI, yet some users prefer to buy a separate word processing program. Why might a user prefer a separate word processing program?

Answers

1. Hardware.
2. Windows, Icons, Menus, Pointer.
3. So that they can be recognised by a variety of software packages.
4. GIF, JPEG, TIFF
5. A toolbar.
6. The Copyright, Designs and Patents Act.
7. The user does not have to start from a blank document but can use a template which already has a lot of the formatting and structure in place.
8. An on-line tutorial.
9. You do not need to search through the pages of a manual: the on-line help is there as part of the program.
10. The data can be protected with passwords.
11. It must be correct and free from errors.
12. Dynamic link.
13. When the data in one document is changed then the linked data in the other document does not change.
14. Any two from word processor, spreadsheet, database and graphics.
15. There is a common HCI.
16. The Computer Misuse Act.
17. The individual about whom data is held on a computer system.
18. Customise the HCI so that the font size is larger or in bold, etc.
19. The Data Protection Act gives John the right to see a printout of his record and insist that any errors are corrected.
20. An individual word processing program will have more advanced features than a word processing program that is part of an integrated package.

How did you do?

Answers correct

1–7 Not very good. You need to go back and learn this topic.

8–12 Reasonable. You know some of the work but look over pages 6–9 before moving on.

13–17 Good. You should move on but go back later and consolidate your knowledge.

18–20 Excellent. You have mastered this topic and can move on.

Word processing 1

Important terms

Enter: text is added

Delete: text is removed

Edit: text is amended

Save: text is saved on a backing store (e.g. hard disc)

Retrieve: text is loaded back into memory from a backing store

Print: hard copy (printout) is obtained.

Top Tip
Learn how to do all the features of word processing described on these pages on the word processing program that you use.

Wordwrap

When a word being entered at the end of a line becomes too long for the remaining space then it automatically comes down to the next line. This is called wordwrap.

Text formatting

Fonts are different styles of text, e.g. Times New Roman, **Geneva**, and **Arial**.

Font size is the height of text measured in points. For example 12-point text is suitable for a letter, while 72 point text is 2.5 cm high and so is suitable for a poster.

The font colour refers to the colours text can be given, eg. black, red, or green. Fonts can be reproduced in many thousands of colours.

Styles are enhancements to the text, e.g. **Bold**, *Italic*, <u>Underline</u>, ~~Strike Through~~, Subscript Superscript etc.

Text alignment

Text alignment (also known as justification), is the way the text is lined up with the left-hand and right-hand margins of the page.

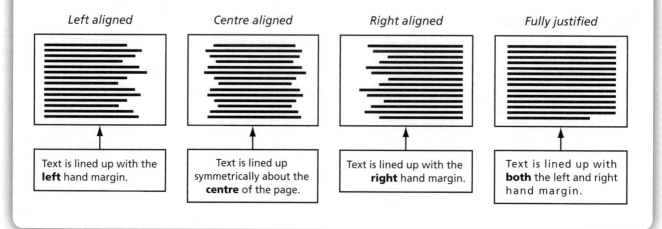

Left aligned	Centre aligned	Right aligned	Fully justified
Text is lined up with the **left** hand margin.	Text is lined up symmetrically about the **centre** of the page.	Text is lined up with the **right** hand margin.	Text is lined up with **both** the left and right hand margin.

Spelling and grammar checks

Spell checks in computer programs can be used to check the spelling of each word in a document. If the word is not in the spell check dictionary then it is highlighted as a spelling mistake.

Spell checks are not perfect: if words such as people's names and places are not in the dictionary then the spell check can wrongly highlight them as errors. Users can choose to skip words that they know are really correct. Users can also add new words to dictionaries.

Grammar checks look for grammatical errors such as 'no capital in a new sentence'.

Tables

A table is a grid of data placed in rows and columns. It is used to present information in an organised form.

Employee	Position	Wage
Ben Lopez	Manager	$25,000
Monica Clinton	Director	$6.9 million
Jennifer Affleck	Clerk	$36,500

Pages

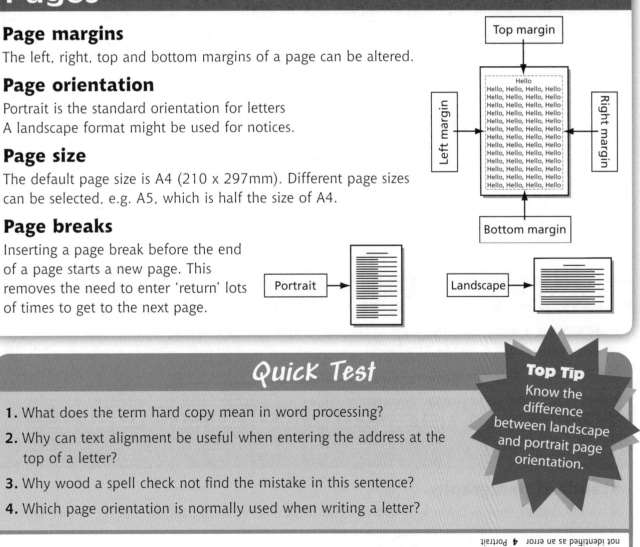

Page margins

The left, right, top and bottom margins of a page can be altered.

Page orientation

Portrait is the standard orientation for letters
A landscape format might be used for notices.

Page size

The default page size is A4 (210 x 297mm). Different page sizes can be selected, e.g. A5, which is half the size of A4.

Page breaks

Inserting a page break before the end of a page starts a new page. This removes the need to enter 'return' lots of times to get to the next page.

Quick Test

1. What does the term hard copy mean in word processing?
2. Why can text alignment be useful when entering the address at the top of a letter?
3. Why wood a spell check not find the mistake in this sentence?
4. Which page orientation is normally used when writing a letter?

Answers 1. A hard copy is a printout of the document **2** Right alignment can be used to move the text to the right-hand margin and remove the need to enter lots of spaces **3** The word 'wood' was entered instead of 'would' but because 'wood' is a proper word it will be in the spell check dictionary and therefore not identified as an error **4** Portrait

Word processing 2

Search and replace

Search and replace allows you to look for a piece of text in a document and replace it with another piece of text.

For example in a story you could change every occurrence of the name of a character from 'Laura' to 'Wendy'.

Care must be taken when using search and replace as, for example, replacing all the occurrences of 'gun' to 'revolver' might also change 'gunge' to 'revolverge'.

To overcome these kind of problems most search and replace features offer a choice of skipping or changing each occurrence.

Top Tip

Try to get a chance to use different word processing programs and explore how to use the features that you use on your own program.

Headers and footers

Headers and footers are used to enter data once. This data will then be shown at the top or bottom of every page of a document.

The data in headers and footers may be titles, page numbers, dates, times etc.

Headers and footers are often used to automatically put page numbers on each page in a long document.

Advantages of headers and footers.

Headers and footers save the user time since the header or footer is inserted only once and then appears on every page. Also if text is inserted or deleted in the middle of a document then the header or footer still remains at the top and the bottom of the pages and does not get out of position.

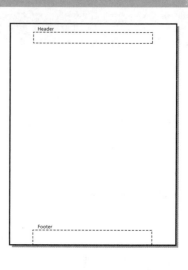

Templates

A template is a document with some of the layout and structure already created, which can be used as the basis for documents over and over again.

CREDIT

Standard paragraphs and standard letters

Standard paragraphs

A standard paragraph is a block of text that has been entered and saved so that it can be used over and over again to save the user time.

For example, a company may have a standard paragraph used in letters to inform job-applicants that they have not been successful.

I am sorry to inform you that you have not been successful at this time but thank you for your interest in our company and good luck in your future career.

Standard letters

A standard letter is a word processing document that can be used over and over again. It can also be personalised with details from a mailing list. The mailing list is usually held in a database file.

Mail merge

The process of inserting details from a mailing list into positions in a standard letter is called mail merge.

The steps required to create personalised letters are:

Step 1 Create a standard letter using a word processing program.

Step 2 Use mail merge to insert details (e.g. name, address, subscription, etc.) into places in the standard letter from a mailing list held in a database file.

Step 3 Print out the personalised letters.

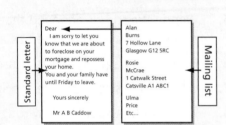

Optical Character Recognition

A scanner can be used to input text documents into a computer. Optical Character Recognition (OCR) software recognises the shapes of characters and converts the scanned image into editable text. OCR is good at recognising typed text but it will not recognise handwritten text if it is too messy or fancy. OCR software can be used to save retyping documents only available on paper.

Printer drivers

A printer driver is software that allows a computer to communicate with a printer. When a new printer is attached to a computer system the printer driver must be installed on the computer. The printer driver translates formatting codes in a document into the correct code for the printer being used.

Quick Test

1. State an item that you would expect to be entered in a footer.

2. Which word processing feature is used to produce personalised letters?

3. What does the acronym OCR stand for?

4. What is a printer driver?

Answers **1.** The date, the time, a piece of text, etc **2** Personalised letters are produced using a feature called mail merge **3** OCR stands for Optical Character Recognition **4** A printer driver is a program that allows a computer to communicate with a printer

Test your progress

Questions

1. What is the difference between deleting and editing text?

2. What is the difference between a hard copy and a backup copy?

3. Give two ways in which text can be formatted.

4. What is the name of the text alignment when the text is lined up with both the left-hand and the right-hand margins?

5. Wendy Weistler is annoyed that when she spell checks her word processing documents her name is always highlighted as a spelling mistake. How can Wendy get round this problem?

6. Name two page orientations used in word processing.

7. Which page size is double the size of A5?

8. Why would a spell check wrongly highlight lots of words as spelling errors in a report on a chemical reaction to make plastic?

9. Give an example of how a school could make use of mail merge.

10. How high are characters that have a point size of 144?

11. How can the pages in a long document be numbered efficiently?

12. What is a template?

13. Why is using OCR software to scan handwriting not usually 100% effective?

14. Winston types the page numbers at the bottom of each page in a long document. Later on he deletes a paragraph and the page numbers move to the middle of the page. Give a solution to his problem.

15. Name two documents required to perform a mail merge.

16. Which type of general purpose package is used to create the standard letter in mail merge?

17. Which type of general purpose package is used to create the mailing list in mail merge?

18. It has been estimated that the average household receives over 100 junk mail letters per year. Why has mail merge contributed to the amount of junk mail that people receive?

19. Wendy has written a letter using a word processor. The letter takes up one full page and spills over to a couple of lines on a second page. What could Wendy do, without deleting any text, so that the letter fits on one page?

20. A student buys a printer at a jumble sale where he sees it working on a computer. He takes it home and connects it to his own computer. However the printer fails to operate. Why would the printer not work with his computer?

Answers

1. To delete text is to completely remove it. Editing changes or amends the text.

2. A hard copy is a printout of the document whereas a backup copy is a second copy of a file in case the original gets damaged or deleted.

3. Text can be formatted by changing the font, font size, font colour or style.

4. Fully justified.

5. Wendy can add her name to the spell check dictionary.

6. Portrait and landscape.

7. A4.

8. The names of chemicals and technical terms would probably not be in the dictionary.

9. To create personalised letters to parents about school events such as parents' nights, school fees, and prize giving.

10. 5 cm.

11. The page number can be entered into a header or footer.

12. A template is a document with a lot of the layout and formatting already in place so that it can be used as a basis for new documents, over and over again.

13. People have varied styles of handwriting and if the handwriting is too messy or fancy then the shapes of the characters will not be recognised.

14. Winston should delete the page numbers from the text and then enter them into a footer. Then they would always appear at the bottom of each page.

15. A standard letter and a mailing list.

16. Word processor.

17. Database.

18. It is very easy for companies to produce personalised letters using mail merge with a mailing list of client's details.

19. Wendy could reduce the font size or make the page margins smaller.

20. The computer needs the printer driver to be installed to operate the printer.

How did you do?

Answers correct

1–7 Not very good. You need to go back and learn this topic.

8–12 Reasonable. You know some of the work but look over pages 12–15 before moving on.

13–17 Good. You should move on but go back later and consolidate your knowledge.

18–20 Excellent. You have mastered this topic and can move on.

Spreadsheets 1

What is a spreadsheet?

A spreadsheet is a grid of cells which can contain numbers, text or formulas.

Each cell has a reference given by its column heading and row number, e.g. cell F5.

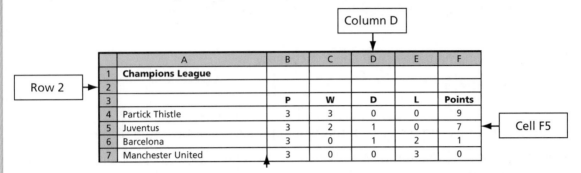

	A	B	C	D	E	F
1	Champions League					
2						
3		P	W	D	L	Points
4	Partick Thistle	3	3	0	0	9
5	Juventus	3	2	1	0	7
6	Barcelona	3	0	1	2	1
7	Manchester United	3	0	0	3	0

Column width and row height of cells can be altered to suit their contents. For example Manchester United would not fit in the normal cell width so the cell has been lengthened.

Formulas

Formulas are used to perform calculations on the data in the spreadsheet.

The arithmetic operations are add (+), subtract (-), multiply (*), and divide (/), e.g. in the above spreadsheet:

	A	B	C
1	3	4	6
2	9	7	2
3	5	1	8

=A3+B2-C3 gives an answer of 4 (= 5+7 − 8)

=A1*B1/C1 gives an answer of 2 (= 3 × 4 ÷ 6)

=(A1+B2+C3)/3 gives an answer of 6 (= (3 + 7 + 8) ÷ 3)

Functions

Functions are built-in formulas that calculate highest values, lowest values, totals, averages, etc.

The functions you need to know for this course are
MAX, MIN, SUM, AVERAGE and IF, e.g. in the above spreadsheet

	A	B	C
1	3	4	6
2	9	7	2
3	5	1	8

= MAX(A1..A3) gives an answer of 9   (The highest value of 3, 9 and 5.)

= MIN(A2..C2) gives an answer of 2   (The lowest value of 9, 7 and 2.)

= SUM(B1..C3) gives an answer of 28   (The sum of 4, 6, 7, 2, 1 and 8.)

= AVERAGE(B1..B3) gives an answer of 4   (The average of 4, 7 and 1.)

The IF function (conditional function) returns one value if a condition is true and another value if a condition is false.

= IF (Condition, True, False)

= IF (A1>10, C1*2, C1*3) gives an answer of 18 since the condition A1>10 is false and C1*3 gives an answer of 18 (= 6 × 3).

CREDIT

Top Tip
An IF function is also known as a conditional function.

Replication

Replication is filling a formula down or across.

CREDIT

Relative cell reference

A relative cell reference is when the cell reference changes according to the row or column that it is copied into.

In this example the formula = A1 + A2 + A3 has been entered into cell A4 and then replicated across row 4. (A1, A2 and A3 are all relative cell references.)

	A	B	C
1	2	4	6
2	5	2	5
3	9	3	7
4	=A1+A2+A3	=B1+B2+B3	=C1+C2+C3

Absolute cell reference

An absolute cell reference is when the cell reference does not change according to the row or column that it is copied into.

	A	B	C
1	2	4	6
2	5	2	5
3	9	3	7
4	=$A$1+A2+A3	=$A$1+B2+B3	=$A$1+C2+C3

Dollar signs are used to make a cell an absolute cell reference, e.g. $A$1.

In this example the formula = $A$1 + A2 + A3 has been entered into cell A4 and then replicated across row 4. ($A$1 is an absolute cell reference, A2 and A3 are relative cell references.)

Top Tip
Know the difference between an absolute and a relative cell reference.

Cells

Top Tip
It is easy to mix up cell formatting with cell attributes. Learn which is which.

Cell formatting

The cell format of a cell is the appearance of a cell, e.g. The width of a cell, the height of a cell, the type of justification.

Cell attributes

The cell attributes are the ways in which the data can be represented in the cell, e.g. the number of decimal places, the way a date is displayed, displaying numbers as currency.

Spreadsheets 2

Cell protection

Cell protection is when the contents of a cell are locked so that the contents can not be changed.

Cells with formulas can be protected so that the formulas are not accidentally or deliberately changed.

Charting

Charting is when cells are selected and the selected data is used to produce a graph.

The types of graph available include bar charts, pie charts and line graphs.

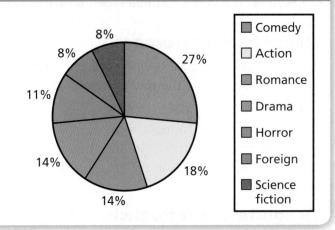

Inserting rows and columns

Sometimes a spreadsheet has to be amended to include an extra row or column of data. This can be done by inserting a new row or column and any formula will adjust automatically.

Quick Test

1. Why does the address of a cell in a spreadsheet include a letter and a number?

2. Give a shorter way of performing the calculation $=D1+D2+D3+D4+D5+D6+D7+D8$.

3. What is replication in a spreadsheet?

4. Name two types of graphs that can be charted in a spreadsheet.

Answers 1. The letter specifies the column and the number specifies the row 2. =SUM (D1..D8) 3. Replication is when a formula is filled across or down
4. Bar graph, pie chart, line graph

Databases 1

Database packages

A database package is a program used to create and organise data in such a way that the data can be easily retrieved and changed.

Advantages of computerised databases:

- they save paper and space compared to manual systems which would use record cards in filing cabinets;
- data can be easily and highly amended without rewriting record cards;
- the records in the database can be quickly sorted into any order;
- databases can be searched quickly to find certain records;
- calculations performed on the data will be accurate. Humans are likely to make mistakes from time to time;
- the data can be made secure by controlling access to files with passwords.

Disadvantages of a computerised database:

- there is a chance that hackers can gain access to confidential data and even make changes to data such as bank balances or exam marks;
- they are liable to virus attacks which can delete files.

Top Tip
Databases are used mainly to store and retrieve data but spreadsheets are used mainly to perform calculations on data.

Fields, records and files

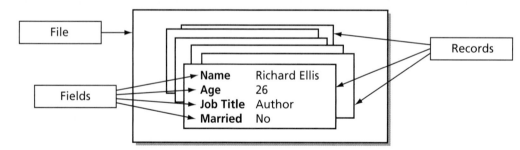

File

A database file is a collection of records on a particular topic. Examples include school databases consisting of records holding student details and second-hand car salesroom databases storing car details.

Organisations such as banks and governments hold huge databases that contain millions of records and require a lot of storage.

Record

A record is the data about one person or thing, e.g. a student record or a car record.

Field

A field is one item of data in a record, e.g. a telephone number field or a mileage field.

Field types

A text field contains characters, e.g. surname, address.

A numeric field contains numbers, e.g. exam mark, age.

A date field contains a date, e.g. date of birth, subscription due date.

A computed field (also known as a calculation field) is calculated from data in other fields using a formula, e.g. a calculation field called 'Pay' could be calculated from the fields 'Hours' and 'Pay per Hour' using the formula:

= [Hours]*[Pay per Hour]

A graphic field contains graphics, e.g. an icon, a smiley face, a student photo.

A key field is a field that contains a unique value in each record so that a particular record can be found by searching for the value in this field, e.g. reference number, account number.

CREDIT

Insert, delete and amend

Database files need to be updated when changes occur. For example a new pupil may come to a school, a pupil could leave the school or a pupil may move house.

Inserting a record

Inserting a record means adding a new record to a database file.

Deleting a record

Deleting a record means removing a record from a database file.

Amending a record

Amending a record is updating or changing the data in a record in a database file.

Top Tip
Sometimes it is necessary to insert a new field so that the records can contain an extra item of data such as a 'Nickname' field or a 'Pet's name' field.

Quick Test

1. Put the following in ascending order of size: record, file, field.

2. Name two field types other than text that are used in a database.

3. A school keeps a database of the pupils on the school roll. Suggest why a record might have to be amended.

4. Name two fields that you would expect to find in a patient's record in a database for a dental practice.

Answers 1. field, record, file 2 Numeric, date, computed or calculation 3 A pupil might change his or her address or telephone number, an exam mark may be entered 4 First name, surname, telephone number, date of next appointment, dental history, etc

Databases 2

Input and output format

The layout of the screen for inputting data can be altered to make it easier to enter data to, e.g. only show the fields into which data is being entered or display the records in columns.

The layout of data to be output can be displayed in different ways, e.g. the records can be printed out in columns, only certain fields may be displayed or the records may be sorted in a certain way.

Searching databases

Searching a database means finding records which meet certain conditions.

The records can be searched via one field or via more than one field.

For example, within an animal database you could search for animals that are reptiles and weigh more than 200 kgs.

A simple search is a search via only one field, e.g. search for records where the 'Salary' field = £30,000.

A complex search is a search via two or more fields, e.g. a search for records where the 'Winner' field = 'Partick Thistle' AND the 'Year' field < 1970.

CREDIT

Top Tip
Questions about selecting records are often answered badly in exams. Always use phrases like 'the Age field <18' or 'the Town field = Chicago' in your answers.

Sorting

Sorting a database means arranging its records in a certain order.

The records can be sorted in ascending (increasing) or descending (decreasing) order.

The records can be sorted via one field or via more than one field.

Simple sort (sorting on one field)

The file below has been sorted in ascending order on the age field.

Name	Address	Age	Pet
P. Collins	2 North Street	13	Parrot
H. Chambers	123 Gaga Drive	19	Dolphin
G. Blackie	100 Treacle Crescent	22	Budgie
.....	.....	.....	.....
T. Gibson	13 Golf Drive	89	Dingo

Records

Complex sort (sorting on two or more fields)

The records are sorted according to the first field. Only if the data in the field is the same for two or more records is the second field used to refine the sort.

The file below has been sorted via two fields.

Field 1 Class field in ascending order.
Field 2 Exam field in descending order.

Top Tip
Find out how to use the sort feature on the database that you use.

Form class	Exam	Date of birth	Hobby
3B	87	120688	Sky diving
3B	72	130988	Archery
3B	56	230488	Jogging
3B	31	091288	Chess
3C	93	290288	Computing
3C	67	301088	Athletics
3C	45	251288	Water polo
3D	89	010189	Reading
3D	70	110588	Sailing
3D	58	250389	Scuba diving
.....	.....	.....	.....

Searching CD-ROMs and the internet

CD-ROMs

Encyclopaedias and databases of information are available on CD-ROM. The information can be accessed using keywords.

For example a CD-ROM encyclopaedia could be searched to find active volcanoes in Europe with keywords such as **volcano**, **active** and **Europe**.

The internet

A virtually endless supply of information is available on the World Wide Web. If a specific website is not known then a search engine can be used to search for information using appropriate keywords.

Popular search engines include Google and Ask Jeeves.

Quick Test

1. A teacher is entering maths marks for students into a database. How can the input format for the database be changed to make this process easier?

2. What is the difference between a simple search and a complex search?

3. What is the term used to describe putting records in a database into order?

4. Wendy wants to find out about flower-arranging classes in her home town of Skegness. She has a computer with internet access but she does not know any websites. How can Wendy find some relevant sites?

Answers 1. The input format can be changed to only show essential fields such as name, form class and maths mark, so that the marks can be entered without scrolling through other fields 2. A simple search is a search via one field. A complex search is a search via two or more fields 3. Sorting 4. She could use a search engine and enter keywords such as **flower, arranging** and **Skegness**

Test your progress

Questions

1. How are the columns in a spreadsheet identified?

2. Which symbols are used for multiplication and division in a spreadsheet?

3. Describe the calculation performed by the function =SUM(A7..D7).

4. The formula, = B5*$C$5-D5 is entered into cell E5 and then replicated into cell E6. What formula results in cell E6?

5. Give the name of a spreadsheet program which is available commercially.

6. What is another name for a conditional function?

7. The price of a mobile phone is entered into a spreadsheet as 149.2. How can the number be displayed as £149.20?

8. State whether a spreadsheet or a database is best for performing calculations.

9. Why is it better to store a supermarket's stock data in a database rather than as a word processing document?

10. What are the items of data that make up a record called?

11. How does the use of a computed field in a database save time when the data is being entered?

12. A shop keeps a database of its stock on computer. Suggest two fields that might be included in the records of the stock database.

13. A database is kept on endangered animals. The records include 'Name', 'Population' and 'Life Expectancy' fields. Why might a record need to be deleted?

14. Why might a record in the endangered animals database in question 13 need to be amended?

15. A teacher keeps data on pupil exam results in a database. The records contain 'Name', 'Form Class', 'First Exam' and 'Second Exam' fields. How can the database be used to find the pupils who passed both exams? (Take 50% as a pass.)

16. Give an advantage of searching for information on the internet as opposed to on a CD-ROM.

17. Give a disadvantage of searching for information on the internet as opposed to on a CD-ROM.

18. A university database has 7,800 student records. Two of the fields are the 'Date of Birth' field and the 'Sex' field.
    How can the database be used to find the youngest female student?

19. An advertising executive uses a spreadsheet to record and process his sales. He uses the charting feature to draw bar charts of the data in the spreadsheet. The data in the spreadsheet is constantly changing.
    Why is a dynamic link preferable to a static link in this situation?

20. A bank keeps its customer details on a computerised database. The bank manager remembers fondly when he was young and everything was kept on paper. He thinks that computer databases are not as secure as databases kept in filing cabinets under lock and key. Give two reasons as to why he might think this.

Answers

1. They are identified by letters, A, B, C, D, etc.
2. Multiplication is "*" and division is "/".
3. The function adds up the contents of the cells A7, B7, C7 and D7.
4. The resulting formula is **=B6*C5-D6**
5. Excel or any other commercially available spreadsheet.
6. An IF function.
7. The cell attributes can be set to currency.
8. A spreadsheet.
9. In a database, records can be sorted and those that meet certain conditions can be selected.
10. Fields.
11. The contents of the field are calculated automatically from a formula and so do not need to be entered by the user.
12. 'Article Name', 'Quantity', 'Price', 'Supplier', 'Re-order quantity', etc,
13. Because an animal becomes extinct or is no longer endangered.
14. Because the population changes or any other suitable answer.
15. Perform a complex search where the 'First Exam' field >=50 AND the 'Second Exam' field >= 50.
16. The internet has vast amount of information available whereas a CD-ROM is more limited.
17. There is a lot of rubbish on the internet and it can take a lot of time to sift through material to find something useful.
18. Select the records where the 'Sex' field = 'Female' and then sort the selected records on the 'Date of Birth' field in descending order: the record for the youngest female student will come first.
19. A dynamic link is preferable since the chart will change automatically when the data is changed whereas it will not for a static link.
20. Computerised databases are vulnerable to hacking and to damage from viruses.

How did you do?

Answers correct

1–7 **Not very good**. You need to go back and learn this topic.

8–12 **Reasonable**. You know some of the work but look over pages 18–25 before moving on.

13–17 **Good**. You should move on but go back later and consolidate your knowledge.

18–20 **Excellent**. You have mastered this topic and can move on.

Graphics

Drawing and painting

A graphics package is a program that is used to produce pictures. There are two types of graphic software — painting and drawing.

Painting graphics store the picture by storing a code for the colour of each pixel that makes up the graphic.

Pixels are the tiny dots that make up the graphic. (The word pixel comes from **pic**ture **ele**ment.)

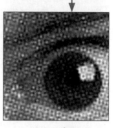

Resolution

High resolution graphics are made up of a large number of small pixels.

This gives a good quality graphic with a lot of detail.

Low resolution graphics are made up of a small number of large pixels.
This gives a poor quality graphic with little detail.

Drawing graphics store the picture as a list of objects (shapes) that make up the graphic.
The objects are shapes such as rectangles, circles and lines.

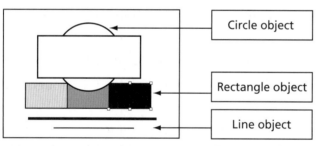

| Circle object |
| Rectangle object |
| Line object |

Top Tip
Talk about the size of the pixels when describing the difference between high and low resolution graphics.

Attributes

The attributes of an object are its features which can be altered, e.g. a rectangle has attributes such as line thickness, line colour and fill colour.

Animation

Animation is the process of producing movement by showing a sequence of still frames. Animation is used in video games, aircraft simulators to train pilots, screen savers and virtual reality systems.

Top Tip
Make sure that you learn a precise definition of terms such as animation. There are many answers that will gain marks in an exam but if your answer is not clear enough you will not be awarded full marks.

Editing graphics

Scale

Scaling a graphic is to changing its size by enlarging or reducing it.

Look at the horse and jockey to see how they have been scaled.

Rotate

Rotating a graphic is turning it through an angle.

Look at the apple to see how it has been rotated.

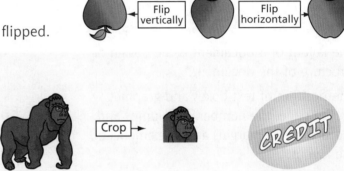

Flip

Flipping a graphic is reflecting it in an axis of symmetry.

Look at the apple to see how it has been flipped.

Crop

Cropping a graphic is trimming its horizontal or vertical edges to show a particular area.

Look at the gorilla to see how it has been cropped.

CREDIT

Scanner

A scanner can be used to input graphics into a computer so they can then be edited. A scanner can also be used to input text on paper: the text can then be transferred to a word processing program for editing. This can save a lot of time when entering a large amount of text that is only available on paper.

Two factors that affect the quality of scanned images are the resolution and the bit depth.

Resolution is measured in dpi (dots per inch), e.g. 3,600 dpi, 4,800 dpi.

Bit depth is a measure of the number of colours that can be detected – a 48-bit scanner can detect more colours than a 32-bit scanner.

Quick Test

1. What is the name given to the dots that make up a graphic?

2. Explain the difference between a painting and a drawing package?

3. Give two ways of making a graphic smaller.

4. What is the implication of a scanner having a high bit depth?

Answers 1. Pixels 2 Paintings are stored as pixels whereas drawings are stored as objects such as rectangles, circles and lines 3 Crop and scale down 4 It can detect a large number of colours

Desk top publishing

What is desk top publishing?

Desk Top Publishing (DTP) software is used to create documents that combine text and graphics. The text and graphics can be created by the user or imported from text and graphics files that have been created before.

DTP is used to produce documents such as newsletters, magazines and brochures.

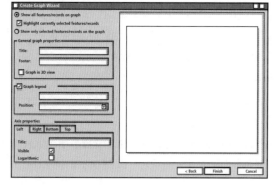

Layout

The layout of a document is the design or structure of the document.

The position of text boxes and graphics on the page, the number of columns and the size of the margins are all elements of the layout.

Top Tip

Wizards and templates come up again in other topics. Make sure that you know what they are and can give a good description of them.

CREDIT

Wizards and templates

Wizards

A wizard is a dialogue between users and programs that guides users through a task. Wizards can be very useful when doing a difficult task or a task that you have never done before.

For example, a graph wizard can guide a user through the task of creating a graph. The user would be asked a series of questions such as:

What title do you want for the graph?

Which type of graph do you want?

What is the label for each axis?

Templates

Templates are used to help users set up new documents. A template has an outline of the structure of a new document already set up. The template can be used as the basis for a document over and over again.

This example has a formatted title and two columns. This template forms the basis for a document.

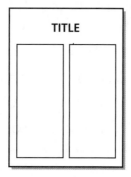

Text

Enter text

Text can be entered into a document using the computer keyboard.

Import text

Text can be inserted into a document by selecting a file which has already been created in a word processing application.

For example, a newspaper reporter may submit text files that are imported into the final newspaper in a DTP program.

Text wrap around graphics

Text can be set to flow around a graphic in different ways. This can make the document more attractive and prevent text from covering up a graphic or vice versa.

The Apple

The apple, The apple, The apple, The apple, The apple, The apple, The apple, The apple, The apple, The apple, The apple, The apple, The apple, The apple, The apple,

Graphics

Import graphics

Graphics can be inserted into a document by selecting a file which has already been created in a graphics application or has been captured using a scanner or a digital camera.

Scale and crop graphics

Graphics that have been inserted into a document will usually need to be scaled or cropped to fit the layout of the document.

Scaling is altering the height and/or width of the graphic.

Cropping is trimming the horizontal or vertical edges of a graphic to show a particular area.

Top Tip
Learn the difference between cropping and scaling a graphic.

Add clip art

Clip art is libraries of graphics provided with software that can be added to a document. Clip art can be viewed by category or searched by keywords.

Quick Test

1. What does DTP stand for?
2. Apart from text, name another element of DTP.
3. What sort of questions would a DTP wizard to set up a newsletter ask the user?
4. What is the name of the DTP feature that makes text flow around a graphic instead of covering it up?

Answers 1. Desk Top Publishing 2. Graphics 3. What is the title of the newsletter? How many columns are there in the page? What font is to be used? 4. Text wrap

Test your progress

Questions

1. What is the difference between the pixels between high and low resolution graphics?

2. Would an image of a model on the front of a fashion magazine be created with a painting or a drawing graphics package?

3. Name two attributes of a line tool.

4. How is animation produced on a computer?

5. Name a computer program that makes use of animation.

6. What does 'to rotate an image' mean?

7. Name two objects that could be used in a drawing package.

8. What is a scanner used for?

9. What does 'crop a graphic' mean?

10. Which term describes the number of colours that a scanner can detect?

11. What is desk top publishing?

12. What is a wizard?

13. Which of the following would be created with a DTP package:
    a) an airplane simulator,
    b) a clothes catalogue or
    c) a multimedia encyclopaedia?

14. What is the term used to describe enlarging or reducing a graphic?

15. What is text wrap used for in desk top publishing?

16. What term is used to describe the design and structure of a document?

17. How can a template save the user time when creating a new document?

18. Wendy is buying a new printer for a company that produces commercial magazines using DTP software. One printer she looks at costs £499 and has a specification that includes 9,600 dpi while another printer costs £79 with 2,400 dpi.
    State which printer Wendy should buy and explain your answer.

19. A graphic to head a company newsletter was changed from Graphic A to Graphic B.

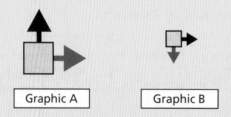

Graphic A   Graphic B

    What features of the graphics package were used to change Graphic A to Graphic B?

20. *The Daily Bugle* newspaper is produced using a DTP package. The newspaper editor insists that the journalists submit their articles as word processing files and not on paper.
    Why does the editor insist on receiving the articles in this form?

Answers

1. High resolution graphics have smaller pixels than low resolution graphics.
2. Painting.
3. Thickness, colour, pattern, etc.
4. Animation is produced by showing a sequence of images.
5. A simulator, video game, etc.
6. To turn the image through an angle.
7. A circle, rectangle, line, arrow or textbox.
8. A scanner is used to input graphics into a computer.
9. Cropping a graphic is trimming its edges.
10. The bit depth.
11. Desk top publishing is the production of documents that consist of text and graphics.
12. A wizard is a guide through a difficult or new task through a dialogue between the computer software and the user.
13. A clothes catalogue.
14. Scaling.
15. Text wrap is used to make text flow around an image rather than covering it up.
16. The layout.
17. The user does not need to start from a blank document but can use a template that already has a lot of the structure and layout already in place.
18. Wendy should buy the high resolution (9,600 dpi) because good quality printouts are required in this situation and the higher cost is unavoidable.
19. The features used are scaling (reduction) and rotate (90° right).
20. The word processing files can be imported directly into the DTP document and will not have to be typed in.

How did you do?

Answers correct

1–7 Not very good. You need to go back and learn this topic.

8–12 Reasonable. You know some of the work but look over pages 28–31 before moving on.

13–17 Good. You should move on but go back later and consolidate your knowledge.

18–20 Excellent. You have mastered this topic and can move on.

Presentation and multimedia 1

What is multimedia?

Multimedia is a description of computer systems that use text, graphics, video and sound.

Slide show presentations are often multimedia. Multimedia applications include encyclopaedias and language teaching programs.

Hardware

As well as the basic computer and keyboard, multimedia systems require items of hardware to store the large files associated with multimedia and to provide the graphics, video and sound elements.

Top Tip

Remember that multimedia consists of text, graphics, video and sound but desk top publishing consists of only text and graphics.

Sound card

A good sound card can be used to input high-quality sound from a microphone and to output high-quality sound to speakers. External speakers can add to the quality of the sound system.

Graphics card

A good graphics card can be used to provide a high resolution display with a large number of colours.

CD (Compact Disc)

CDs have high storage capacities and are therefore suitable for storing the large files associated with multimedia systems.

DVD (Digital Versatile Disc)

DVDs have much larger storage capacities than CDs and therefore can contain better quality graphics, video and sound. However DVDs are more expensive than CDs.

Multimedia

Entering text

Text is usually entered with the keyboard but text files that have already been created can be imported directly into a multimedia document.

Capturing graphics

Graphics can be captured using a scanner or a digital camera.

CREDIT

Capturing video

Video can be captured using a digital camcorder.

Capturing audio

Sound can be captured with a microphone and a sound card.

Other sources

Text, graphics, video and sound can be obtained from other sources such as libraries of materials on CD-ROM, clip art and the internet.

Hyperlinks

A hyperlink is a piece of coloured text or graphic that when clicked provides a link to another slide.

CREDIT

Wizards

These are often used to guide users through a series of steps to create a slide-show.

Templates

Presentation packages provide templates so that slide-show creators do not need to start from scratch. These templates will already have some layout and formatting.

Presentation packages

Presentation packages are used to create slide-shows with multimedia content.

For example, PowerPoint can create a slide-shows with animation of text and sound when images appear.

Linear linkage of slides

A linear linkage of slides is when the slides are displayed from the first slide to the last slide in the same order as they were created.

Presentation and multimedia 2

Multimedia authoring package

A multimedia authoring package is a program that allows the creation of a stand-alone multimedia application, such as an encyclopaedia, on CD.

Stand-alone means that the application can run by itself without the authoring package that was used to create it.

A multimedia authoring package has more extensive programming options, (e.g. pull-down menus, command buttons, scroll bars) than a presentation package.

Top Tip

A lot of students don't explain the difference between a presentation package and a multimedia authoring package very well. Learn good descriptions of both of these.

Animation and video

Animation is the simulation of movement by showing a sequence of images.

Video consists of real moving pictures captured by a digital camcorder or a similar device.

Quick Test

1. What are the elements of a multimedia presentation?

2. Do you use a presentation package or a multimedia authoring package to create a stand-alone application?

3. The creator of a slide show presentation decides to allow the user to repeat the show by putting a link from the last slide to the first slide. How can this be achieved?

4. Name two devices that can be used to capture graphics for a multimedia presentation.

Answers 1. Text, graphics, video and sound 2. A multimedia authoring package 3 The creator can put a hyperlink on the last slide that links to the first slide 4 A scanner and a digital camera

Web page creation

What is the world wide web?

The world wide web (www) is a vast amount of multimedia information stored on the internet in the form of websites. These websites are accessed by their web addresses but can be found by using search engines and entering appropriate keywords.

Websites

A website is a collection of web pages with hyperlinks between them.

For example the BBC website (www.bbc.co.uk) has a home page from where the user can follow links to TV, sport, news, etc.

Search engines

Search engines use keywords entered by the user to display lists of websites containing these keywords.

For example websites about the weather in Paris could be searched for with keywords such as **Paris**, **forecast** and **weather**.

Google and Ask.com are popular search engines.

Browsers

A browser is a program that displays web pages and allows the user to **surf** the internet. Popular browsers include Internet Explorer and Netscape Navigator.

Web page creation

HTML (Hypertext Markup Language)

HTML is a programming language used to create web pages. It uses tags to describe the items on the page. For example, the following HTML codes use the title tag to set the page title to 'SG Success' and the bold tag to display a line of text in bold.

    <title>SG Success</title>

    This line is in bold.

Writing web pages in HTML is very difficult and time-consuming as it requires a lot of technical expertise and experience.

Web page editors

Web page editors are used to make the process of creating web pages much simpler and to speed up the process. The web page can be created using a set of tools: this frees the creator from the technical difficulties of using HTML code.

Popular web page editors include Dreamweaver and FrontPage.

Top Tip

Open any web page in Internet Explorer and choose Source on the View menu to see the HTML code for the page.

General purpose packages

Some general purpose packages, such as Microsoft Word, allow the user to create a normal word processing document and then save it as a web page.

Tables, audio and video

CREDIT

Tables

Tables are used to organise data in a web page by displaying it in a grid of rows and columns.

Audio

Sound files can be embedded in a web page but this substantially increases the size of the web page. Alternatively the creator can put a hyperlink to the sound file on the page.

Video

Similarly video files can be embedded in a web page or a hyperlink to the video file can be created.

Hyperlinks and hotspots

CREDIT

Hyperlinks

Links between web pages are achieved by the use of hyperlinks. These are usually pieces of coloured text that users can click to activate the links.

Hotspots

A hotspot is an active area of the screen that triggers an event when the user moves their mouse pointer over it. The mouse pointer usually changes from an arrow to some other icon such as a hand or a musical note.

For example, hotspots could be used in a Christmas web page so that hovering over various presents on a Christmas tree would trigger the playing of Christmas carols.

Top Tip
Know the difference between a hyperlink and a hotspot.

Quick Test

1. What does HTML stand for?

2. What is a browser?

3. Why are most websites these days created using a web page editor rather than HTML?

4. What is the name given to a piece of coloured text on a web page which, when clicked, opens another page?

Answers 1. Hypertext Markup Language 2 A program that displays web pages and allows the user to surf the world wide web 3 A web page editor allows web pages to be created much faster than using HTML as it does not require any technical knowledge of the language instructions 4 A hyperlink

Expert systems

What is an expert system?

An expert system is a program that mimics the decision or diagnosis of a human expert. Expert systems are used in areas such as medicine, law and machine repair. They are not necessarily used as an alternative to a human but as an extra opinion which may be acted on. Some people are concerned that there are dangers involved in the increasing use of expert systems in our lives and of the ethical and legal issues stemming from their use.

The components of an expert system

The knowledge base

The knowledge base contains a set of facts and rules about the problem. For example, a medical expert system would contain facts about which symptoms are features of which diseases.

An example of a rule in a medical expert system could be:

> IF Temp>101 AND Skin=Spots AND Throat=Dry
> THEN Disease=Malaria.

The knowledge base can contain thousands of facts and rules so it can take a lot of time to gather and enter the data into the expert system.

The facts and rules are provided by human experts on the relevant subjects.

Top Tip

The exam often asks for a definition of the three components of an expert system so make sure that you know them. These are the knowledge base, the explanatory interface and the inference engine.

The explanatory interface

The explanatory interface is the component of the expert system which asks questions of the user. For example, a medical expert system would ask the user questions such as: 'What is the patient's temperature?' or 'Does the patient have a rash?'.

The inference engine

The inference engine draws a conclusion or makes a diagnosis based upon the facts and rules that are stored in the knowledge base.

An expert system can also provide an explanation of how it arrived at its conclusion.

Advantages and disadvantages of an expert system

Advantages
Rare and unusual cases that a human might not know about can be included in the knowledge base of a medical expert system.
The conclusion or diagnosis can be made more quickly by the expert system than by a human.
Consistent results are obtained whereas a human can be more erratic in reaching a conclusion.

Disadvantages
Many people have concerns about machines may be making important or even life-threatening decisions. For example, many people would be worried if an expert system was being used in areas such as air traffic control or medical diagnosis.
A computer system is inflexible and lacks common sense whereas people are more adaptable and intuitive in their approach.

Top Tip

When asked to give an advantage or disadvantage avoid one word or very brief answers. Give full answers that provide reasons or explanations in order to demonstrate that you understand how complex an area this can be.

Quick Test

1. Name an area of human activity where an expert system might be used.

2. Name the three main components of an expert system.

3. Give an example of a rule that could be stored in a knowledge base for an expert system which gave advice on car repair.

4. Why might a patient be concerned that expert systems are used in medicine to make decisions about his/her treatment?

Answers 1. Expert systems are used in areas of human activity such as medicine, law, car repair and oil exploration **2** The three components of an expert system are the knowledge base, the explanatory interface and the inference engine **3** Black smoke coming out of the exhaust AND a high oil temperature is a symptom of oil leakage or any rule which links a symptom with a mechanical flaw **4** A patient might be concerned that a machine is being used to make a life-or-death decision

Test your progress

Questions

1. Which element of a multimedia system is missing from this list: text, video, graphics?

2. Why are multimedia encyclopaedias stored on CD-ROMs or DVDs and not floppy discs?

3. Give one difference between a presentation package and a multimedia authoring package.

4. Name a device that can be used to capture video for a multimedia presentation.

5. How is animation achieved on a computer system?

6. Give an example of a presentation package which is available commercially.

7. The mouse pointer hovers over an article on a web page showing pictures of articles for sale. The mouse pointer changes to a hand and the item can be dragged into a shopping basket.
    Is this an example of a hyperlink or a hotspot?

8. Embedding video files in a web page can vastly increase the size of the web page. What is a possible solution to this problem?

9. What name is given to an active area of a web page that triggers an event when the mouse pointer is moved over it?

10. For what purpose are tables used in web pages?

11. How are links between pages achieved in a website?

12. Give an example of a commercially-available web page editor.

13. What is the function of the inference engine of an expert system?

14. Who provides the information in the knowledge base of a legal expert system?

15. Which component of an expert system asks questions of the user?

16. Give two advantages of an expert system.

17. Give two disadvantages of an expert system.

18. Computerised programs are used for the teaching of French in many schools.
    In one program everyday scenes are shown on the screen such as a kitchen, classroom, beach, etc. When the user clicks on an object in the scene the program displays the name of the object in French, plays an audio file to speak the name, and shows a video of the object moving.
    What makes this program multimedia?

19. Sam works as a web page designer for a chain of health clubs. He has been asked by his boss to include hotspots in his web pages.
    How can you tell that a web page includes hotspots?

20. A Scottish farmer has a herd of 200 dairy cows. When a cow is sick he calls out the vet which costs him a lot of money each time.
    Which type of computer software could the farmer make use of which might save him money in vet's fees?

Answers

1. Sound
2. Multimedia requires high capacity storage media to hold text, graphics, video and sound.
3. A multimedia authoring package creates a stand-alone application and has more extensive programming capabilities.
4. A digital camcorder.
5. Animation is achieved by showing a sequence of images.
6. PowerPoint or any other suitable answer
7. Hotspot
8. A hyperlink to the video file can be created.
9. A hotspot
10. Tables are used to display information in an organised fashion in rows and columns.
11. Hyperlinks are used to link pages in a website.
12. Dreamweaver, FrontPage or any other suitable answer.
13. The inference engine comes to a conclusion or makes a diagnosis based upon the rules and facts in the knowledge base.
14. Lawyers and legal experts
15. The explanatory interface
16. Rare cases can be included, faster diagnosis/conclusion than a human.
17. Expert systems are inflexible and there is mistrust that a machine is making a decision.
18. The program is multimedia because it contains text, graphics, sound and video data.
19. Moving the mouse pointer over an active area of the screen will trigger an event.
20. The farmer could make use of an expert system to help with the treatment of his cows.

How did you do?

Answers correct

1–7 Not very good. You need to go back and learn this topic.

8–12 Reasonable. You know some of the work but look over pages 34–41 before moving on.

13–17 Good. You should move on but go back later and consolidate your knowledge.

18–20 Excellent. You have mastered this topic and can move on.

Electronic communication

E-mail (electronic mail)

E-mail is the process of sending information electronically between computers.

Users are identified by e-mail addresses to send and receive e-mails. Example of e-mail addresses include: Andy@Hotmail.com or Sugar@Universal.co.uk.

Attachments

CREDIT

A basic e-mail is a simple text message. However, users often wish to send files along with e-mails. An attachment is a file that is sent along with an e-mail message. Attachments can be word processing documents, graphic or even programs. Attachments can be used to do things like send photographs or share music files with friends.

Advantages
E-mails arrive almost instantly while the post can take several days.
E-mails do not incur the expense of stamps.
The same e-mail can be sent at once to a group of people in an address book.

Disadvantages
E-mails can include viruses that do damage to computer systems.
E-mails can only be sent to people who have e-mail addresses.

Netiquette

Netiquette is the name given to the rules of good behaviour when sending e-mails. Netiquette is a shorthand way of saying 'network etiquette'.

There are many rules of netiquette which can be found on the internet by entering **netiquette** into any search engine. A few of the more important rules are given opposite.

Top Tip
Learn at least two rules of netiquette since they are often asked in the exam.

1. E-MAILS SHOULD NOT CONSIST ENTIRELY OF CAPITAL LETTERS. THIS IS CALLED 'SHOUTING'.

2. E-mails should not be sent if they contain angry or inflaming remarks such as 'Try to do better next time or you are fired'. Sending such e-mails is called flaming.

3. Sending junk e-mails is not good manners. This is called spamming.

4. E-mails should not be too formal. Unlike a conventional letter you are not expected to use terms such as 'Dear Sir' or 'Yours sincerely'.

5. Don't waste other people's time. For example, repeatedly sending funny stories downloaded from the internet or messages that are unnecessarily lengthy wastes time.

Text messaging

Devices such as mobile phones and palmtop computers can send text messages to each other.

SMS (Short Messaging Service) is a system used to send text messages between mobile phones. Most mobile phones do not have full keyboards and so a language of abbreviations has grown to make the creation of messages quicker. For example someone might send 'C U L8R' instead of 'see you later'.

Fax

A fax machine scans a paper document and translates the picture into a code of binary numbers.

The binary numbers are then transmitted over the telephone line to another fax machine which converts the numbers back into a picture and produces a printout.

Faxes are normally used to transmit fairly small amounts of data such as orders or invoices.

Top Tip
The name 'fax' comes from the word facsimile, which means 'exact copy of'.

Quick Test

1. Why might the owner of a digital camera use attachments in his/her e-mails?

2. Jane wishes to send the same letter to eighty pupils in her year group at school. What is the advantage of e-mail compared to the traditional postal service in this situation?

3. What does it mean to shout in an e-mail?

4. Reporters for a national newspaper have a choice of sending their stories to the editor by e-mail or by fax. Why is e-mail much better in this situation than sending faxes?

Answers 1. The graphics files of the photos taken by the digital camera can be sent as e-mail attachments **2** E-mails can be sent to a group of people in an address book unlike the postal service where eighty letters would have to be sent, at the cost of eighty stamps **3** SHOUTING IS USING ALL CAPITAL LETTERS IN AN E-MAIL. THIS IS AN EXAMPLE OF SHOUTING. **4** The stories on a fax arrive on paper and need to be re-entered into a computer in preparation for publication. E-mails can be copied and pasted into the main newspaper document.

LANs and WANs

What is a computer network?

Stand-alone

A stand-alone computer is one which is not connected to any other computers. Nowadays most organisations and even homes don't operate with stand-alone computers but link computers together to form a computer network.

Two or more computers that have been connected so that they can share resources and communicate with each other make up a computer network.

For example, a school may have a computer network so that students can share printers and access programs and files stored on a central computer.

Administrator

LAN (Local Area Network)

A LAN is a computer network where the computers are in a room, building or other relatively small area. The computers are usually connected together with transmission cables but sometimes wireless connections are used.

WAN (Wide Area Network)

A WAN is a computer network where the computers are spread over a large area, such as groups of buildings, towns or even countries. The computers are connected using telecommunication channels. A device called a modem is required to convert the signals from the computers into a format that can be transmitted down the telephone line.

Top Tip
Note that WAN stands for WIDE Area Network and not WORLD Area Network. This is a common mistake. Avoid it!

Network terms

Security

Security on networks is important and access to users' files is usually protected by the use of usernames and passwords. Networks can be at risk of virus attacks: anti-virus software can help to reduce this risk.

Encryption is another method of security: confidential data is encoded so that even if it is hacked into then it is useless to the hackers.

Multi-access

Multi-access is where two or more users can access the data on a single computer at the same time.

Teleworking

Teleworking uses computer networking technology to allow users to work at home.

Advantages
At home you can work the hours that suit you.
Working at home avoids the stress of an office environment.
The time and expense of travelling to work is saved.

Disadvantages
The equipment and resources of the office are not available at home.
There is sometimes less chance of promotion because you are not part of the office environment.
You can become socially isolated and may miss the company of friends at work.

Client/server network

CREDIT

A client/server network is a computer network where there are two different types of computers called servers and clients.

The servers are powerful computers which provide network resources and the clients are workstation computers that make use of the network resources.

A file server is a computer with a lot of storage capacity that stores and controls access to files on the network.

A print server manages the printing on the network by storing a queue of files to be printed.

Top Tip
Know the names of these two types of server and be able to describe their functions.

NIC (Network Interface Card)

A NIC is a circuit board which a computer needs to allow it to be connected to a computer network. The NIC converts the signals from the computer into a form that can be broadcast over the network. It also receives signals from the network and feeds them back into its computer.

Quick Test

1. What do the terms WAN and LAN stand for?

2. Why is a computer network more at risk of a virus attack than a stand-alone computer?

3. What is a server on a client/server network?

4. Which item of hardware must be in a computer that is to be used on a LAN?

Answers 1. Wide Area Network and Local Area Network 2. If a stand-alone computer is infected by a computer virus then only that computer is infected but on a network the virus can spread to all the other computers on the network 3. A server is a computer, such as a file server or a print server, that provides a network resource 4. A network interface card

The internet

What is the internet?

The internet is a global network of individual computers and networks.

The world wide web

The world wide web (www) is a virtually limitless amount of multimedia information stored on websites on server computers on the internet.

This information can be accessed by entering the address of the website into a browser or by using a search engine.

(ISP) Internet Service Provider

An ISP is a company that provides access to the internet. Most individuals using a computer from their homes subscribe to an ISP for a monthly payment.

Examples of ISPs are AOL (America On Line) and Pipex.

CREDIT

Types of connection

Dial-up

Dial-up is a slow internet connection. Each dial-up session needs a new connection to the ISP. This can cause a wait of a few minutes.

Broadband

Broadband is a very fast internet connection that is tens of times faster than a dial-up connection. The other advantage over dial-up is that a broadband connection is always on so there is no waiting time to connect. However broadband has the disadvantage of being more expensive than dial-up.

The internet

Internet-ready

An internet-ready computer is a computer that already has the required hardware and software for the computer to be connected to the internet.

On-line

A computer that is on-line is one that is connected to the internet.

Search engine

When the address of a suitable web page is not known the internet can be searched by entering keywords into a search engine such as Google or Ask.com.

Top Tip
Try out different search engines on the internet and compare the results they give for the keywords **glossary** and **computing**.

Wireless

CREDIT

Wireless connections provide freedom of movement. Also the absence of cabling makes for a less cluttered and safer working environments. Wireless connections are typically slower than cable connections.

Bluetooth

Bluetooth allows devices to communicate with each other over a short distance using radio waves. For example a user could use Bluetooth to create a personal wireless network between a mobile phone, a laptop and a printer.

Wi-Fi (Wireless Fidelity)

Wi-Fi uses special areas called hotspots in places such as airports and trains to allow computers to be wirelessly connected to the internet.

Video conferencing (Credit)

CREDIT

Video conferencing is a system of video and sound communication between computers.

Advantages
People can have virtual meetings without incurring the time and expense of travelling and accommodation.
Disabled and sick people who may have difficulty travelling can meet more easily.

Disadvantages
If the connection is not fast enough then the pictures and sound can be of poor quality.
Video conferencing lacks the personal touch of meeting people, making eye contact, shaking hands, and so on.
Extra hardware, such as video cameras, good quality speakers and microphones, are needed.

Downloading software

Software downloaded from the internet can be classified as follows:

Freeware

Freeware is software that is completely free and never has to be paid for.

Shareware

Shareware is software that can be used for free for a trial period after which it must be paid for or deleted.

Commercial

Commercial software is never free and must be paid for before it is downloaded.

Top Tip
Learn the differences between freeware, shareware and commercial software since questions based on this content are frequently asked in the exam.

Test your progress

Questions

1. What does the 'e' in e-mail stand for?

2. What is an attachment in an e-mail?

3. Explain why a virus sent in an e-mail can quickly spread to thousands of computers.

4. Give one way of making the composition of a text message quicker.

5. Describe how a document is sent over the telephone line from one fax machine to another.

6. What is a stand-alone computer?

7. How could a virus infest a stand-alone computer since it is not connected to any other computers?

8. A school classroom has twenty stand-alone computers and one printer. What could the teacher do to allow all of the pupils to obtain printouts of their work?

9. Is a network of computers in a school an example of a LAN or a WAN?

10. How can the security of a user's files be maintained on a computer network?

11. Describe the function of one type of server on a client/server network.

12. What does NIC stand for?

13. What is meant by teleworking?

14. What are the financial savings gained by video conferencing?

15. Give one disadvantage of a broadband connection over a dial-up connection.

16. A user spends a lot of time downloading music from the internet.
    Is a broadband or a dial-up connection best suited to this purpose?

17. Richard wants to find information on the life of Elvis Presley for a music project at school. Suggest some keywords that he could enter into a search engine?

18. **WHICH THREE LAWS OF NETIQUETTE DOES THIS QUESTION BREAK OR ARE YOU TOO LAZY TO ANSWER AS USUSAL?**
    YOURS SINCERELY
    MISS QUESTION SETTER

19. Rosaleen works as an advertising contractor for a jazz magazine based in London. In her work she contacts clients and takes placements for adverts. Rosaleen finds travelling and the stresses of the office very wearing and would like to leave London and live in Scotland. How could Rosaleen live in Scotland and continue to do the same job?

20. Software that can be downloaded from the internet is classified as freeware, shareware and commercial. Sophie is interested in using software to create her own screen savers. She wants a professional-level program but would like to try it out before she buys it. State which type of software Sophie should download and explain your answer.

Answers

1. Electronic

2. An attachment is a file that is added to an e-mail and sent along with it.

3. Once the virus has infected one computer, it can spread through the e-mail address book to many other e-mail users and the process is then repeated.

4. Abbreviations or predictive text messaging can be used.

5. The document is converted into binary numbers which are then sent down the telephone line and converted back into the document at the receiving fax machine.

6. A stand-alone computer is one that is not connected to any other computer.

7. The virus could get into the computer via a floppy disc, memory stick, etc.

8. The teacher could copy the files to be printed onto a memory stick or some other device and input them into the computer connected to the printer.

9. LAN

10. Files can be made secure by using usernames and passwords to control access.

11. A file server stores and controls access to user files and programs; a print server manages the network printing by storing a queue of files to be printed.

12. Network Interface Card

13. Teleworking uses computing technology and the internet to allow people to work from home.

14. Travelling expenses, accommodation costs, hiring of conference rooms, etc.

15. Broadband is more expensive than dial-up.

16. Broadband because it is a faster connection and music files are large.

17. Elvis, Presley, biography, music.

18. Shouting, flaming and being too formal.

19. Rosaleen could live in Scotland and work from home using e-mail and other communication technology to contact the jazz magazine and her clients.

20. Sophie should download shareware since it should be better quality than freeware and she will have a trial period before she has to pay for it.

How did you do?

Answers correct

1–7 Not very good. You need to go back and learn this topic.

8–12 Reasonable. You know some of the work but look over pages 44–49 before moving on.

13–17 Good. You should move on but go back later and consolidate your knowledge.

18–20 Excellent. You have mastered this topic and can move on.

Commercial data processing 1

The data processing cycle

Large organisations collect and process a large volume of data every day.

They use computers to process this data because they are faster and more accurate than humans.

Hardware

A very powerful computer with a fast processor and large storage capacity is called a mainframe computer. A mainframe computer is needed to cope with the large volume of data that has to be processed in commercial data processing.

The data processing cycle is the name given to the steps in which data is collected, input, processed and output.

The paper document used to collect the data is called a source document.

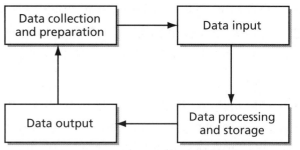

Data and information

Data is the term for numbers, text and graphics stored on a computer.

Information is the term for data when it is given meaning.

For example, the data item 180901 stored on a computer could mean almost anything.

If you are told that it is a date of birth (18th September 2001) then it is given meaning and becomes information.

Top Tip
Remember the difference between data and information by learning the formula INFORMATION = DATA + MEANING.

Collection and input of data

There are a wide variety of methods of entering data automatically into a computer system.

Bar codes

Bar codes are patterns of lines of varying thicknesses which contain data. They are input into computers using bar code scanners. Bar codes have check digits to detect errors when they are read.

Bar codes are used in supermarkets and book shops.

OMR (Optical Mark Recognition)

Marks are made on cards (mark sense cards) which are read by an OMR document reader.

OMR is used in the National Lottery and multiple choice exams.

OCR (Optical Character Recognition)

Typed or hand-written letters and numbers are read directly by an OCR document reader.

OCR can be used to save retyping documents only available on paper or to enter data from forms.

MICR (Magnetic Ink Character Recognition)

Characters written in special magnetic ink that are read by a MICR reader.

MICR is mainly used on cheques as magnetic ink is difficult to forge.

Magnetic stripes

Magnetic stripes are used on credit cards, bank cards, etc, to allow the details on the card to be read automatically.

A smart card is a plastic card about the size of a credit card with an embedded microchip that can be loaded with data and used for telephone calls and electronic cash payments.

A check digit is a number which is calculated from the digits in the number and attached to the end of the number.

When the number is entered into the computer, it performs a recalculation of the check digit. The computer then compares the calculated check digit with the input check digit. If the input check digit and the recalculated check digits are different then an error has occurred.

Top Tip

Learn what the acronyms OMR, OCR and MICR stand for.

Methods of output of data

- Data can be displayed on a screen.
- Data can be sent to a printer to produce a hard copy on paper.
- Data can be saved as a file onto a backing store such as a hard disc or tape.

Quick Test

1. What does MICR stand for?
2. Why does reading OMR documents produce fewer errors than reading OCR documents?
3. What is on a bar code to make sure that it has been read properly?
4. What is a hard copy?

Answers 1. Magnetic Ink Character Recognition 2. OMR only has to recognise a mark where OCR has to recognise the shapes of characters 3. A check digit 4. A printout of a document

Commercial data processing 2

Buying and selling goods

EFTPOS (Electronic Funds Transfer at Point of Sale)

In EFTPOS the customer buys goods with a credit or debit card instead of cash.

A computer link is made to the customer's bank which checks whether there is enough money in the customer's account to pay for the goods.

If there is enough money then the price of the goods is transferred from the customer's bank account into the shop's bank account almost immediately.

E-commerce

E-commerce uses computer technology to buy and sell goods.

Companies use the internet to advertise and sell their products.

Advantages

• The entire world becomes a market place.
• Businesses do not need to invest in shops, staff etc.

Disadvantages

• There is a chance of credit card fraud.
• Only customers who have the necessary technology can be contacted.

Top Tip
Study this topic and then try and answer the quick test questions.

Access and use of information

CREDIT

Direct/Random access

Data on a disc can be read by direct random access. This means that the read/write head in the disc drive can go straight to any part of the disc.

Sequential access

Data on a magnetic tape is read by sequential access. This means that other data on the tape must be read in order to get to the required data.

Single entry, multiple use

The data held on a database need only be entered once to then be used in a variety of ways. For example, only certain fields such as 'name' and 'maths mark' could be shown in a report on exam results. Another report might show certain fields sorted on a particular field and so on.

Multi-user database

A multi-user database is a database that can be accessed and updated by two or more users. This is important in an office where several people are using the same customer database.

Sales of customer lists

Companies may use customer details held on their databases to make money by selling the details to other organisations. For example, a finance company could sell its customer lists to companies that sell luxury goods.

Jobs in Computing

Systems analyst

A systems analyst observes and analyses a computer system and advises upon which hardware and software is required to implement specific tasks.

Programmer

A programmer writes, tests and maintains computer programs.

Computer engineer

A computer engineer installs, maintains, upgrades and repairs the hardware of a computer system.

Network manager

A network manager creates, deletes and amends user accounts. He/she also installs new programs and maintains printers.

Top Tip
Learn the difference between validation and verification.

Validation and verification

CREDIT

Validation

Validation of data means checking that data is sensible or possible. Programs will ask for invalid data to be re-entered.

A range check will only accept a value in a certain range. For example, if a month is entered as a number then it must be in the range of 1 to 12.

A length check will only accept data of a certain length. For example, if a date of birth is entered then it must be six digits long.

Verification

Verification of data means checking it to make sure that it is accurate.

To do this, the same data is entered twice. The program then compares both versions and highlights any differences which are then corrected.

Quick Test

1. What does EFTPOS stand for?

2. Apart from writing new programs, what else does a programmer do?

3. Which term describes the selling of goods over the internet?

4. What is the name of the process of entering data twice to check its accuracy?

Answers 1. Electronic Funds Transfer at Point of Sale 2 He/she tests and maintains existing programs 3 E-commerce 4 Verification

Test your progress

Questions

1. Why is a mainframe computer used in commercial data processing?

2. What does OMR stand for?

3. Copy and complete the equation INFORMATION = DATA +

4. What is the job title of a person who maintains software?

5. What type of access is used to read data from a magnetic tape?

6. What type of access is used to read data from a disc?

7. Is it validation or verification when a program asks the user to re-enter an age because they keyed in 199?

8. What is the name of a card that has a microchip to store and update data?

9. Why is MICR used on checks and not OCR?

10. What is the name of the person who has the job of repairing a damaged disc drive in a computer?

11. What are the four steps in the data processing cycle?

12. Apart from displaying the data on a screen, give another way of outputting data from a computer system.

13. What validation can be done when entering a percentage exam mark?

14. What is a multi-user database?

15. Why are passwords usually required to be at least six characters long?

16. What is the advantage of EFTPOS to a customer in a supermarket?

17. Give a disadvantage to a customer of using credit cards to pay for goods.

18. The post office spends lots of hours and money on sorting letters by hand using their address and post code.
    Why does the post office not use OCR software to sort all the mail?

19. Each week millions of people play the national lottery by choosing their numbers on a ticket which is read by an OMR system.
    Why is OMR used on lottery tickets instead of the shop assistant typing in the numbers?

20. Prunella buys a lot of her hair and skin care products over the internet using e-commerce. She never uses her credit card to pay for the goods. Instead she pays the bill by sending a cheque.
    Suggest why Prunella would choose to pay by cheque rather than with her credit card.

Answers

1. A mainframe is used because it is a powerful computer with a large memory that can process a vast amount of data.
2. Optical Mark Recognition
3. INFORMATION = DATA + MEANING
4. A programmer
5. Sequential
6. Direct/random
7. Validation
8. A smart card
9. MICR characters are printed with special magnetic ink. They are therefore much harder to forge. (OCR which simply reads by light.)
10. A computer engineer.
11. Data collection and preparation, data input, data processing and storage, data output
12. Sending the data to a printer or sending the data to a file on a backing store
13. The mark can be rejected if it is not in the range 0 to 100 and can be entered again
14. A database that can be accessed by two or more users at the same time
15. If the password is too short it can be too easy for it to be discovered.
16. The customer does not need to carry large amounts of cash.
17. The customer can be vulnerable to credit card fraud.
18. Using OCR would be much faster but people have different styles of handwriting and some handwriting is illegible so OCR cannot decipher it as well as a human sorter.
19. The numbers can be entered quickly, without typing errors.
20. Credit card fraud is a problem when buying goods over the internet and paying by cheque is safer.

How did you do?

Answers correct

1–7 Not very good. You need to go back and learn this topic.

8–12 Reasonable. You know some of the work but look over pages 48–51 before moving on.

13–17 Good. You should move on but go back later and consolidate your knowledge.

18–20 Excellent. You have mastered this topic and can move on.

Industrial applications /automated systems 1

Stationary robots

Stationary robots are fixed to a point on the floor.

They are used in car assembly plants to weld car parts together.

Anatomy of a robot arm

The parts of a robot arm have the same names as a human arm.

elbow → wrist

shoulder →

gripper

waist

Top Tip
Learn the names of the parts of a robot arm.

Tool/end effector

A tool, sometimes known as an end effector, is fitted at the end of the wrist to allow the robot arm to perform a useful task. End effectors include grippers, welders and paint spray guns. A gripper is used to move objects from one place to another, a welder welds pieces of metal together and a paint spray gun is used to paint objects.

Degrees of freedom

CREDIT

The number of degrees of freedom of a robot arm is the number of different ways in which it can move.

Typically a robot arm has seven degrees of freedom:
   it can turn at the waist;
   it can rise at the shoulder;
   it can bend at the elbow;
   it can perform four movements at the wrist
   — roll, pitch, yaw, and extend.

Roll is when the wrist rotates.

Pitch is when the wrist moves up and down.

Yaw is when the wrist moves from side to side.

Extend is when the wrist reaches out.

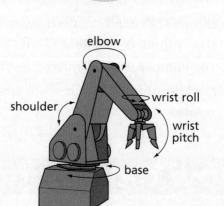

elbow

shoulder

wrist roll

wrist pitch

base

Mobile robots

Mobile robots can move around. An example of their use would be in warehouses to carry goods to trucks for delivery.

Safety

When humans are working in the same area as robots there are safety issues to consider.

Safety precautions include flashing lights on the robots, barriers enclosing the area in which the robots work and sound alarms that go off when humans approach.

There are two main methods of guiding a mobile robot by following a path: white lines and electric wires.

White lines

White lines are painted on the floor and the mobile robot is fitted with a light sensor to detect the light emitted from the lines.

Electric wires

Electricity is passed through wires laid out on the floor and a magnetic field sensor is fitted to the base of the mobile robot to detect the magnetic field emitted from the wires.

Top Tip

When asked about how a mobile robot finds its way around a floor, talk about the sensors as well as the lines.

Programming robots

Programming

A program can be written with a set of instructions that the robot carries out.

Lead through (or copycat)

An operator moves the robot arm through the movements that are required to perform the task. The movements are recorded and can be played back over and over again.

Control language

A control language is a programming language which has instructions that are specific to the needs of an automated device. The instructions correspond to movements of parts of the machines, e.g. rotate waist 180°.

ROM software

Some robots have their programs stored in a ROM (Read Only Memory) chip.

The programs in the ROM chip do not have to be loaded up from a disc, keep their contents when the power is switched off and cannot be easily changed or deleted.

Intelligent robots

Intelligent robots are robots that are programmed to behave as if they have a form of intelligence. These robots can adapt automatically to their environment.

Quick Test

1. What is the name of the two parts of a robot arm that rotate closest to the elbow?

2. Which wrist movement would be used to tighten a bolt?

3. Would electrical wires or white lines be best for the mobile robots to follow in a factory where the floor gets dirty?

4. What does the term 'lead through' mean?

Answers 1. Wrist and shoulder **2** Roll **3** Electrical wires because they will not be affected by dirt. The robots will not be able to follow white lines if they are covered with dirt **4** A human moves the robot arm through the required movements which can be recorded and played back repeatedly

Industrial applications /automated systems 2

Process control

Sensors

Sensors measure quantities such as heat, light, movement, pressure and radiation.

Analogue data

Data measured by sensors such as temperature and pressure is analogue data because it changes smoothly.

Digital data

The data stored in a computer is digital: it changes in small steps.

A to D converter

CREDIT

An analogue-to-digital converter is required to change analogue data, e.g. input from a temperature sensor, into digital data so that it can be entered into a computer.

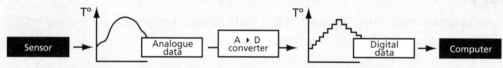

A digital-to-analogue converter is required to change digital data stored on a computer into analogue data so that it can be output to devices such as electric motors, that require analogue data.

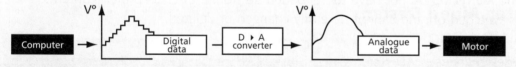

Feedback

Feedback is data sent back to the controlling computer from sensors.

Open loop

In an open loop control system there is no feedback.

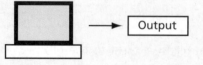

Closed loop

In a closed loop control system there is feedback from sensors.

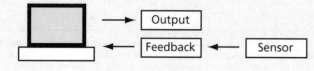

Top Tip
Make sure that you know the difference between an open loop and a closed loop.

Interface

A computer processor operates at a faster speed and uses different codes for data than the peripheral devices attached to it.

An interface is a component placed between the processor and a peripheral device to compensate for these differences.

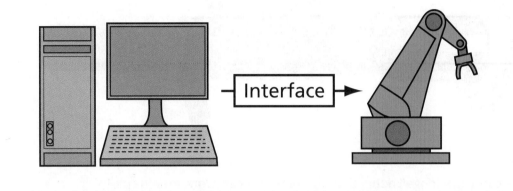

Embedded system

Devices such as washing machines, microwaves and DVD recorders contain microchips equipped with programs that control the devices. These are called embedded systems.

An embedded system is a combination of hardware and software that performs a dedicated task as part of a larger machine.

CAD, CAM and simulators

CAD (Computer Aided Design)

CAD is used to produce 3-D drawings on computer.

Architects and car designers use CAD systems.

CAM (Computer Aided Manufacture)

CAM is when a computer is used to control the manufacture of an article.

The use of robots in a car assembly line is an example of CAM.

Top Tip
Memorise the meaning of the acronyms CAD and CAM.

Simulators

A simulator is the use of a computer system to represent a real situation such as flying an aircraft or performing a surgical operation.

Virtual reality is a form of simulation where virtual reality gloves can be used to input movement from the user. Users can be shown rsulting images via virtual reality helmets.

Advantages
- Training can take place in a safe environment.
- Extreme or rare situations can be created.
- Savings can be made on the cost of materials such as fuel.
- No damage is made to expensive equipment.

Advantages and disadvantages of using robots

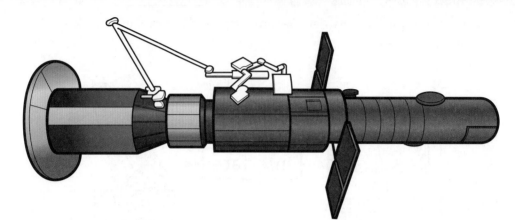

Advantages

- Robots can work longer hours than humans and can work more rapidly.
- Robots can work in dirty and dangerous situations such as on the seabed and in space.
- Savings can be made on human wages.
- Robots do not go on strike or have days off sick or go on holiday.
- Robots can perform tasks more accurately than humans and never get tired.
- Savings can be made on the heating and lighting of factories because robots can work in less comfortable environments.

Disadvantages

- The initial installation of robots can be very expensive.
- Humans may lose their jobs as a result of the automation of factories with robots, although some people may be retrained to program and maintain the robots.

Quick Test

1. Is the volume of a gas in a reaction chamber an example of analogue or digital data?
2. What is the difference between an open loop and a closed loop process control?
3. Would CAM or CAD be used to produce drawings for a new athletics stadium?
4. Give two advantages of using robots in space exploration.

Answers 1. Analogue **2** A closed loop has feedback from sensors while an open loop does not **3** CAD **4** Robots can work in dangerous conditions, don't need air supplies, can lift heavy loads and other suitable answers

Test your progress

Questions

1. What is a stationary robot?

2. Which part of a robot arm performs a yaw movement?

3. Describe a pitch movement.

4. Name an end effector that could be used by a robot arm in a car assembly plant.

5. Describe a safety precaution that is used when humans are working near robots.

6. Why is lead through sometimes called copycat?

7. What is a control language?

8. Give an advantage of storing a program to control a robot on a ROM chip.

9. Give one disadvantage of storing a program to control a robot on a ROM chip.

10. What is a mobile robot?

11. Give one example of data that is analogue.

12. What is the difference between analogue and digital data?

13. What is an embedded system?

14. In a computer system for a house a light goes on when the owner approaches the front door at night. What type of sensor is required for this system?

15. What is feedback?

16. Does an open loop or a closed loop system have feedback?

17. What do the acronyms CAD and CAM stand for?

18. A washing machine is an example of a closed loop system.
    Why is it more efficient for a washing machine to operate a closed loop system rather than an open loop system?

19. In Japan simulators are used to train young doctors in brain surgery. The simulators allow the doctors to practice difficult operations without any danger to patients.
    What are the other advantages of using a simulator instead of operating on real patients?

20. The introduction of robots in a car assembly plant can cost the company millions of pounds in capital expenditure and subsequent running costs (maintaining the robots, etc.). How can the company justify this huge expenditure?

Answers

1. A robot which is fixed to the floor

2. The wrist

3. An up and down movement of the wrist

4. Gripper, welder, paint spray gun or any other suitable answer

5. Flashing lights can be put on the robots, the robots can be fenced in, or warning sounds can be triggered when humans approach.

6. A human operator performs the required movements to do a task on the robot arm and then the robot copies these movements over and over again.

7. A special purpose programming language, e.g. to program a robot arm.

8. The program does not need to be loaded from disc, cannot be deleted and the program keeps its contents if the power is switched off.

9. The program cannot be deleted.

10. A robot that moves around.

11. Heat, pressure, weight or any data that changes smoothly and not in small steps.

12. Analogue data changes smoothly whereas digital data changes in small steps.

13. The hardware and software that performs a dedicated task as part of a larger machine

14. Movement sensor

15. Feedback is data that is picked up by a sensor and sent back to the controlling computer.

16. Closed loop

17. Computer Aided Design and Computer Aided Manufacture

18. The sensors used in a closed loop system (e.g. temperature sensor) provide feedback to the controlling program which then sends out appropriate signals to the devices in the washing machine (e.g. turn the heater on/off).

19. Rare and unusual cases can be practiced without waiting for a real patient to become available, money can be saved on drugs and other materials required for the operation.

20. Money is saved on workers' wages and less money is spent on heating and lighting costs for human workers. Also the robots can work twenty-four hours a day, seven days a week and are more productive, accurate and efficient than human workers.

How did you do?

Answers correct

1–7 Not very good. You need to go back and learn this topic.

8–12 Reasonable. You know some of the work but look over pages 58–63 before moving on.

13–17 Good. You should move on but go back later and consolidate your knowledge.

18–20 Excellent. You have mastered this topic and can move on.

Hardware 1

The components of a computer

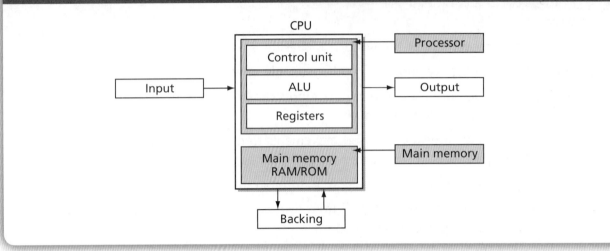

CPU (Central Processing Unit)

The CPU is made up of a processor and main memory.

The processor fetches and executes the program instructions from main memory.

Main memory stores the program instructions and associated data that is currently being processed.

The processor has three components: the control unit, the ALU and registers.

Control unit

The control unit sends out signals to manage the fetching and execution of instructions.

ALU (Arithmetic Logic Unit)

The ALU carries out arithmetic and performs logical decisions such as AND, OR, NOT, etc.

Registers

Registers are individual storage locations on the processor chip. They hold items of data that are required by the processor to perform its functions.

For example, a register called the accumulator temporarily stores the results of calculations performed in the ALU.

Main memory is made up of RAM and ROM.

RAM (Random Access Memory)

RAM can be written to and it is this part of main memory. When they are run, programs are loaded from backing store into this. Any data associated with the program is also loaded into RAM.

RAM is volatile. This means that it loses its contents when the user switches off the computer.

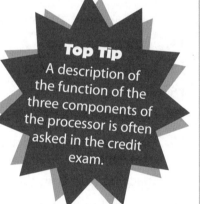

Top Tip
A description of the function of the three components of the processor is often asked in the credit exam.

CREDIT

ROM (Read Only Memory)

The programs stored in a ROM chip are put there at manufacture, after which the contents of ROM never change. ROM is used to store part of the computer's operating system, called the BIOS, which is executed when the computer is switched on.

Unlike RAM, if the computer is switched off, then ROM retains its contents.

Top Tip
Learn the difference between RAM and ROM.

Backing store

Programs and data files are stored permanently on backing store.

Types of computer

Mainframe

A mainframe is a large powerful computer used by organisations that need to store and process large amounts of data. A mainframe computer can cost millions of pounds.

Desktop

A desktop computer is a computer that is too heavy to be easily carried around and is designed to be used at a desk. It will usually have a QWERTY keyboard and a mouse. A QWERTY keyboard gets its name from the first line of letters on the keyboard.

Laptop

A laptop computer is a computer that is portable (easily carried around). It will have a QWERTY keyboard and a touchpad as input devices since. The display is usually a flat TFT (Thin Film Transistor) screen.

Palmtop/PDA

A palmtop or PDA (Personal Digital Assistant) computer is a small portable computer that can easily be held in the hand. It will usually have a special pen, called a stylus, to write on a touch sensitive screen.

Health risks

Damaged eyesight

Spending long periods of time staring at a computer screen can have a bad affect on eyesight. One remedy to this problem is to use a screen filter.

RSI (Repetitive Strain Injury)

Some people spend hours every day typing data into a computer. Over a period of months or years this repeated action can cause damage to the fingers and wrists.

Backache

Sitting in an uncomfortable position over a computer can cause backache. In this respect it is important to sit in a comfortable seat.

Hardware 2

Input devices

Keyboard (QWERTY): used to key in data.

Mouse: used to move a pointer and select.

Touchpad: used to move a pointer and select.

Scanner: used to capture images.

Digital camera: used to capture photographs.

Digital camcorder: used to capture video.

Graphics tablet: used to enter graphics by writing on a horizontal surface with a special pen called a stylus.

Touch-sensitive screen: the user touches an area on the screen to choose from a menu.

Joystick: used to move a pointer or object on the screen.

Microphone with a sound card: used to capture sound.

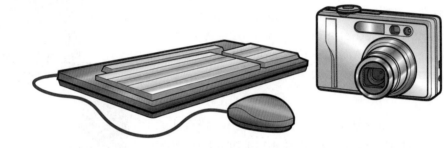

Output devices

Printers

An inkjet printer creates a printout by squirting tiny droplets of quick-drying ink onto paper.

A laser printer uses a laser to make an image of electric charges. The image on a drum is then transferred onto paper using a powder called toner.

Display screens

A monitor (Cathode-Ray Tube) is a heavy and bulky display.

An LCD (Liquid Crystal Display) is a low-power flat-screen display.

A TFT (Thin Film Transistor) is a flat-screen display created with tiny transistors.

Other output

A flat-bed plotter uses a pen to create an image on a horizontal sheet of paper.

A loudspeaker with a sound card is used to output sound.

Backing store devices

Magnetic devices

Magnetic devices store data by coding it on the magnetic coating of a disc or tape.

A floppy disc drive stores the data on flexible discs which are 3.5 inch in diameter. The capacity of the disc is 1.4 megabytes.

Hard disc drives are rigid discs that typically have a capacity in the range 20 gigabytes to 1 terabyte.

Magnetic tape drives can have tape that is several hundred metres long and typically have capacities in the range of 10–100 gigabytes.

Top Tip
Devices which store data permanently are called backing store devices even although they perform both input and output of data. They are not called input or output devices.

Optical devices

Optical devices use lasers to read and write data that is coded on the surface of the disc in lands (peaks) and pits (holes).

CD-ROMs (Compact Disc Read Only Memory) hold data that can be read but the disc cannot be written to. Typically they hold around 700 megabytes of data.

CD-Rs (Compact Disc Recordable) can be written to only once. The recorded data can then be read as often as required but not rewritten.

CD-RWs can be read from and written to over and over again.

DVD, DVD-R and DVD-RW are optical discs that have higher capacities than CD discs. Their capacities range from 4.7 to 17 gigabytes.

Solid state

Solid state devices are devices with no moving parts.

USB flash memory is compact and portable and typically has a capacity of 1–2 gigabytes.

Types of access

CREDIT

Direct/random access

This is access to data stored on disc that can be read immediately from any part of the disc. This type of fast access is used when speed is important.

Sequential access

This is access to data stored on tape where other data must be read through in order to get to the required data. This type of slow access can be used when speed is not important.

Capital costs/running costs

Capital costs

These are the initial costs when items are bought. These costs include items of hardware, software, furniture, etc.

Running costs

These are the costs incurred in replacing and maintaining items.

Voice recognition

Voice recognition is increasingly being used to input data to computers. Also, speech synthesis can be used to output data instead of conventional screen displays. Both of these methods are often used with computer systems for blind or deaf people.

Examples of hardware devices

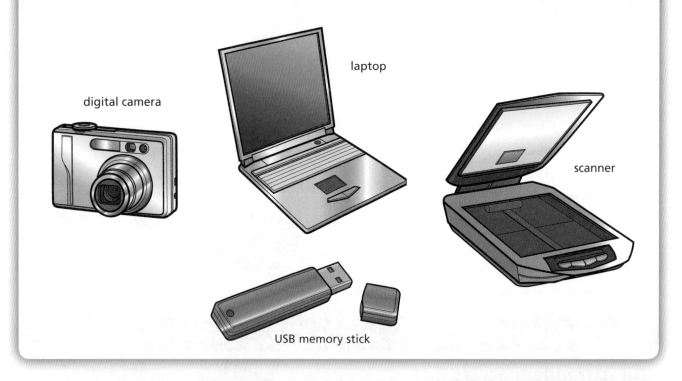

digital camera

laptop

scanner

USB memory stick

Quick Test

1. Name two types of printer.
2. Name a backing store device suitable for transferring large files between two computers.
3. Which type of access is required of the backing store device that holds the customers' data on a bank's cash line system?
4. What are the running costs of an inkjet printer used in a family home?

Answers 1. Inkjet and laser 2. USB stick or CD-RW or DVD-RW 3. Direct access 4. Paper, ink cartridges, repair costs electricity

Test your progress

Questions

1. What does ALU stand for?

2. What is the function of a register?

3. Which component of the processor is responsible for managing the fetching and execution of instructions from main memory?

4. Name the two components of main memory.

5. Put these types of computer into ascending order of size: laptop, mainframe, palmtop, desktop.

6. What does ROM stand for?

7. Describe one possible health hazard when working at a computer for long periods of time.

8. Which of the following types of computer are portable? laptop, mainframe, palmtop, desktop.

9. How does a QWERTY keyboard get its name?

10. Name one backing store device.

11. Which prints faster: an inkjet or a laser printer?

12. Does a DVD or a CD have the higher storage capacity?

13. Name two devices that can be used to capture images for a computer system.

14. Why would magnetic tape not be used to store up-to-the-minute details of client bookings in a travel agent?

15. What are the capital costs of setting up a computer system to run a library?

16. What is another name for random access?

17. Which has faster access to its data: magnetic disc or magnetic tape?

18. A bank decides to improve its cash machine system by providing voice output at its high street cash points.
    Suggest a disadvantage of voice output in this system.

19. A secretary is sitting at a computer entering text into a word processing document.
    While the text is being keyed in, is it stored in RAM or ROM? Explain your answer.

20. Polly is a successful author of children's books. She has a laptop computer which she uses to word process her stories. Polly is considering buying a palmtop computer to replace the laptop since palmtops are more portable than laptops.
    Is it a good idea for Polly to switch from a laptop to a palmtop to write her books? Explain your answer.

Answers

1. ALU stands for Arithmetic Logic Unit.
2. A register stores a single item of data in the processor.
3. The control unit is responsible for managing the fetching and execution of instructions from main memory
4. Main memory is made up of RAM and ROM.
5. Palmtop, laptop, desktop, mainframe.
6. ROM stands for Read Only Memory.
7. Answers include backache, bad eyesight, repetitive strain injury of the wrists and fingers.
8. Palmtop and laptop are portable.
9. QWERTY gets its name from the first line of letters on the keyboard.
10. Hard disc, floppy disc, DVD, CD, flash memory, magnetic tape, etc.
11. A laser printer prints faster than an inkjet printer.
12. A DVD has higher storage capacity than a CD.
13. A digital camera, scanner or camcorder.
14. Magnetic tape has sequential access that is too slow for this situation.
15. The capital costs would include buying computers, printers, barcode scanners, office furniture and software.
16. Another name for random access is direct access.
17. Magnetic disc has faster access than magnetic tape.
18. Background noise could be a problem and there may be a lack of security as other people could overhear transactions.
19. RAM. RAM is random access memory and can be written to. ROM is read-only memory and cannot be written to.
20. It is a bad idea. Although the palmtop is smaller and lighter it does not have a full QWERTY keyboard so that entering text would be much slower than with a laptop.

How did you do?

Answers correct

1–7 Not very good. You need to go back and learn this topic.

8–12 Reasonable. You know some of the work but look over pages 66–71 before moving on.

13–17 Good. You should move on but go back later and consolidate your knowledge.

18–20 Excellent. You have mastered this topic and can move on.

System software

Program files and data files

Program file

A program file is a set of instructions to solve a problem.

Data file

A data file is a file of data, such as a word processing document or records in a database file, created by a program.

Low Level Language (LLL)

Machine code is a computer's own programming language. It is written in binary numbers.

In the early days of computing all programs were written in machine code.

It is very difficult and time consuming to write programs in machine code as all instructions and data have to be in binary code.

Top Tip
Think about whether the programming language that you use in this course is interpreted or compiled or does both.

High Level Language (HLL)

A high level language is a programming language that uses everyday words in the instructions.

Shown below are a few high level language instructions.

Let Length=Inputbox("Please enter the length").   Let Breadth=Inputbox("Please enter the breadth").

Let Area=Length*Breadth   Picture1.Print "The area of the rectangle is: ";Area

Common features

A HLL uses everyday English for its keywords.

Complex arithmetic can be performed in instructions using +, -, *, /.

There are built-in functions that perform maths, logic, etc.

The instructions can be grouped into items called procedures.

One HLL instruction translates to many machine code instructions.

Need for translation

Computers only understand instructions in their own programming languages. Therefore high level language instructions have to be translated into machine code to be executed.

CREDIT

Translators

A translator is a program that translates a high level language into machine code.

The HLL code is called source code and the machine code is called object code.

Interpreters

An interpreter translates a high level language program into machine code and executes it as the program is run.

Compilers

A compiler translates a high level program into a stand alone machine code program which can run independently of the compiler.

Comparison of interpreters and compilers.

- A compiled program runs faster than an interpreted program since an interpreted program takes time to translate the instructions at run time.

- A compiled program uses up less memory than the equivalent interpreted program since independent machine code is produced with the compiler. The interpreted program always requires the interpreter program and the source to be loaded into main memory at run time.

- An interpreted program is easier to correct and edit while the program is being developed as once the changes have been made the program can be run again immediately. A compiled program must be re-compiled before it can be run again.

Utilities and program features

A utility program is a program that is used to protect and maintain a computer system.

A **disc repair** utility is used to recover files from a damaged disc.

A **file compression** utility reduces the size of files so that they take up less space.

An **anti-virus** utility protects against virus infection.

Portable

A program is portable if it is easily adapted to run on a different computer system from the one on which it was originally written.

Robust

A program is robust if it does not crash easily when the user inputs something silly.

Quick Test

1. What is machine code?

2. Which translator, an interpreter or a compiler, produces a program that runs faster?

3. Name two utility programs.

4. A user enters a letter into a program when it is expecting a number and the program crashes. Is the program robust?

Answers **1.** Machine code is a programming language with instructions in binary that are written in the computer's own language **2.** A compiler **3.** Disc repair, file compression, anti-virus **4.** No, because it crashes easily with unexpected input

Operating systems

What is an operating system?

An operating system is a large program that manages the hardware and software of the computer system.

Examples of operating systems are Windows, Linux and Mac OS.

Top Tip

You are not expected to know the names of commercial operating systems in the exam but you are expected to know what an operating system is and its functions.

Functions of an operating system

An operating system can be considered as being made up of several components, each of which performs a function.

CREDIT

HCI

The operating system provides a Human Computer Interface (HCI) for the user to communicate with by inputting commands.

File management

This component manages the saving and loading of files to and from disc. It does this by creating a directory which holds information such as the names and addresses of files stored on the disc.

Memory management

This component allocates program and data files to areas of main memory.

Input/output

This component manages the input of data from input devices and the sending of data to output devices.

Process management

This component controls the allocation of the processor time when it is shared between two or more tasks, e.g. running a chess program and playing a music file at the same time.

Error reporting

It is important for the OS to report errors such as 'no disc in disc drive' or 'printer out of paper'.

Foreground/background printing

Foreground/background printing is where the processor is shared between the foreground task of dealing with input from the user and the background task of sending data to the printer. The user can continue to use the computer for his/her next task while printing goes on in the background.

Processing modes

Batch processing

In this processing mode, the data is collected and then entered into the computer in one go. Then the data is processed by the computer without any human input or interaction.

For example, students doing a multiple choice exam enter their answers onto special cards. Later on all the cards are entered into a computer system and processed in one go.

Top Tip
The term processing mode means how the data is being processed, e.g. batch processing, interactive processing or real time processing.

Interactive processing

In this processing mode there is a dialogue between the user and the computer.

For example, when using a word processing program, the user enters some data or makes a menu choice, the computer responds, the user enters some more data and so on. In this situation there is an interaction between the user and the computer program.

Real time processing

In this processing mode, the data is entered and processed without any time delay. For example, a booking system requires a booking to be entered and processed immediately so that no-one else can make the same booking. In this way multiple bookings are avoided.

Hierarchical filing systems

A hierarchical filing system is one where the disc can contain multiple directories (folders) which themselves can contain sub-directories which themselves can contain sub-directories and so on.

The main directory is called the root directory.

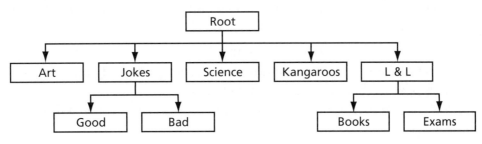

Advantages

• It is easy to find and manage files by grouping them in appropriately named folders.
• Files can have the same name provided they are not in the same directory.

Quick Test

1. Name the operating system that you use on your school computer.
2. Name one function of an operating system.
4. Which processing mode is used by an aircraft pilot simulator?

Test your progress

Questions

1. What is a program file?

2. What name is given to the computer's own programming language?

3. Give the name of a programming language which is available commercially.

4. Which type of programming language uses everyday language for its keywords?

5. Which programming language has the following program been written in?

11010011	0001011111000010
00010010	1000010100000111
10001100	1111101101010011

6. Give two common features of high level languages.

7. What is a more formal name for a folder in a filing system?

8. Give one advantage of a compiler over an interpreter.

9. What is a utility program?

10. What does it mean to say that a program is portable?

11. What is an operating system?

12. Name two functions of an operating system.

13. What is meant by the term real time processing?

14. Give the name of a commercially available operating system.

15. How can foreground/background printing save a user time?

16. How does the file management component of the operating system keep track of where files are saved on a disc?

17. What is the name of the processing mode where data has to be entered and processed immediately?

18. A programmer is writing software to control the flight of the space shuttle. When developing the program he uses an interpreter to translate the program into machine code and then a compiler to translate the completed program.
    Why does the programmer use an interpreter and a compiler at these stages of program development?

19. Hussein uses a hierarchical filing system to store his files on the hard disc of his computer. He has six files called 'Letter' stored in different directories. Hussein wants to store all his 'Letter' files in the same directory so that he can find them more easily.
    What must Hussein do to store his six 'Letter' files in the same directory?

20. Airlines use a booking system where customers can either book their flights through a travel agent or over the internet. Why is batch processing not a suitable processing mode for an airline flight booking system?

Answers

1. A program file is a set of instructions to solve a problem.
2. Machine code
3. Visual Basic, C, Java
4. A high level language
5. Machine code
6. The keywords are in everyday English, one HLL instruction translates to several machine code instructions, instructions can be grouped into procedures, etc.
7. A directory
8. The final program runs faster and there is less memory used up as the source code is not required at run time.
9. A program used to protect and maintain a computer system
10. A portable program is easily adapted to run on a different computer system.
11. An operating system is a large program that manages the hardware and software of the computer system.
12. Error reporting, memory management, file management, etc
13. Real time processing is a mode of processing where the data collected must be input and processed without any time delay.
14. Windows, Linux, Mac OS.
15. The user does not have to wait for the printing but can continue with his/her next task while the printing goes on in the background.
16. The file management system keeps a directory of the names and addresses of the files on the disc.
17. Real time processing
18. The interpreter makes editing the source code easier than the compiler while the program is being developed. However, the compiler is used for the completed program because it will run faster than an interpreted program because no translation is needed at run time.
19. He must rename the files so that they all have different names.
20. Processing the collected data in a batch at a point in the future would result in multiple bookings of the same seats.

How did you do?

Answers correct

1–7 Not very good. You need to go back and learn this topic.

8–12 Reasonable. You know some of the work but look over pages 74–77 before moving on.

13–17 Good. You should move on but go back later and consolidate your knowledge.

18–20 Excellent. You have mastered this topic and can move on.

Low level machines 1

Units

A bit is a binary digit (1 or 0).

A byte is a group of eight bits (e.g. 10001011).

A kilobyte (Kb) is 1,024 bytes (2^{10} bytes).

A megabyte (Mb) is 1,024 kilobytes
= 1,048,576 bytes (2^{20} bytes).

A gigabyte (Gb) is 1,024 megabytes
= 1,073,741,824 bytes (2^{30} bytes).

A terabyte (Tb) is 1,024 gigabytes
= 1,099,511,627,776 bytes (2^{40} bytes).

Representing text

Each character is given a unique code in binary.

ASCII (American Standard Code for Information Interchange)

The ASCII system is a standard used for text where each character is represented in an 8-bit binary code. The first bit has a special error checking purpose and the remaining 7 bits represent the code. This allows the ASCII system to represent 128 characters.

Control characters

Some of the ASCII codes are not used to represent characters but are special control codes.

Examples of control characters are 'return' (moves the cursor to the start of the next line) and 'tab' (moves the cursor to the next tab stop).

Character set

The character set is the complete group of characters that the computer system can represent.

Representing numbers

Integers

Integers are positive and negative whole numbers. They are represented in a computer system in the binary number system.

For example the number 217 is represented by 11011001.

```
128 64 32 16 8 4 2 1
 1  1  0  1 1 0 0 1  = 128 + 64 + 16 + 8 + 1 = 217.
```

Floating point numbers

Real numbers include integers and decimal fractions. They are represented in a computer system in floating point notation. A floating point number consists of a decimal fraction part called the mantissa and a power part called the exponent.

Mantissa   Exponent

For example $1101011010101 = \mathbf{0.1101011} \times 2^{13}$

Advantage
Very large and very small numbers can be represented in a small number of bits.

Disadvantage
Accuracy may be lost since the mantissa is rounded off to a set number of significant figures.

Representing graphics

Bit-mapped graphics (painting) store the graphic by storing a binary code for the colour of each pixel (picture element) that make up the graphic.

Storage requirements of graphics

In black and white graphics, the state of each pixel is stored in 1 bit.
Black can be represented by a 1 and white by a 0.

For example the graphic of the girl shown below contains $480 \times 500 = 240{,}000$ pixels.
Each pixel requires 1 bit of storage.
Therefore the total storage requirements
= 240,000 bits
= 240,000/8 bytes
= 30,000 bytes.

Top Tip
You will only be asked to calculate the storage requirements for black and white graphics. Don't worry about colour graphics for this type of question.

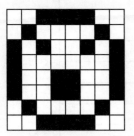

```
00111100
01000010
10100101
10000001
10011001
10011001
01000010
00111100
```

Picture displayed on the screen

The same picture stored in the computer's memory

500 pixels

480 pixels

Low level machines 2

Addressability

CREDIT

Storage locations

Main memory is made up of a large number (usually millions) of storage locations which hold program instructions and data.

Each location is given a unique address so that the processor can identify it.

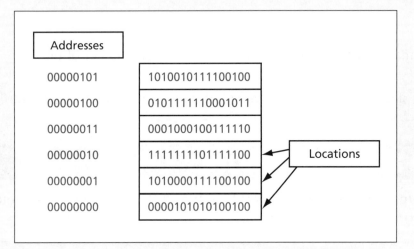

Number of storage locations

The number of storage locations that can be addressed by the processor depends upon the number of bits used for the address.

One-bit addresses can identify two storage locations because $2^1 = 2$.
>   (These are 0 and 1.)

Two-bit addresses can identify four storage locations because $2^2 = 4$.
>   (These are 00, 01, 10, 11.)

Three-bit addresses can identify eight storage locations because $2^3 = 8$.
>   (These are 000, 001, 010, 011, 100, 101, 110, 111.)

Number of bits in address	Number of storage locations
1	$2^1 = 2$
2	$2^2 = 4$
3	$2^3 = 8$
4	$2^4 = 16$
5	$2^5 = 32$
6	$2^6 = 64$
7	$2^7 = 128$
8	$2^8 = 256$
9	$2^9 = 512$
10	$2^{10} = 1024$

Word

The processor does not process 1 bit at a time but transfers groups of bits as a unit.

A word is a group of bits that is transferred as a unit within the processor.

The word size of a processor is the number of bits that it transfers as a unit.

For example a 64-bit processor has a word size of 64 bits.

Quick Test

1. How many bytes are there in a megabyte?

2. What does ASCII stand for?

3. In black and white graphics, how many bits are required to store the state of each pixel?

4. How many addresses can be identified using a 6-bit address?

Answers 1. 1,048,576 **2.** American Standard Code for Information Interchange **3.** 1 bit **4.** 64

Test your progress

Questions

1. What name is given to a group of 8 bits in a computer system?

2. Put the following terms into decreasing order of size: megabyte, terabyte, byte, kilobyte, bit, gigabyte.

3. How many kilobytes are there in a gigabyte?

4. How many characters can be represented by the ASCII system?

5. How much storage is required to store the following text in ASCII codes: *I passed!*

6. What is the largest integer that can be stored in 1 byte?

7. What term is used to describe a group of bits that is transferred as a unit within the processor?

8. Convert the binary number 01010111 into decimal.

9. Convert the number 166 into binary.

10. Explain how text is represented in a computer system.

11. Give an example of a control character.

12. What is a character set?

13. Describe how bit-mapped graphics are stored in a computer system.

14. In black and white graphics, how many bytes are required to store 2,400 pixels?

15. What does it mean to say that main memory is addressable?

16. How many addresses can be identified using a 7-bit address?

17. If a computer can identify 256 addresses, how many bits are used for an address?

18. Calculate the storage requirements of the black and white graphic shown below. (Give your answer in bytes.)

900 pixels

640 pixels

19. Walter is looking for a new computer system to help him in his work as an engineer. He sees an advert for a computer which has the following specification: 1 Ghz processor, 128-bit processor, 2 Gb RAM and a 160 Gb hard drive, CD/DVD combined drive, 17-inch monitor.
    What is the word size of this computer system?

20. A bird watching club keeps a database of British birds on computer. The database has 1,600 records and each record requires 288 bytes of storage. Calculate the storage requirements of the database in kilobytes.

Answers

1. A byte

2. Terabyte, gigabyte, megabyte, kilobyte, byte, bit

3. 1,048,576

4. The ASCII system can represent 128 characters.

5. 9 bytes. (1 byte for each character including the space and the exclamation mark.)

6. 255. (11111111 = 128 + 64 + 32 + 16 + 8 + 4 + 2 + 1 = 255)

7. A word.

8. 87

9. 10100110

10. Each character is stored in a unique code in one byte. ASCII is a widely used standard system for text.

11. Tab, return, end of file or any other suitable answer.

12. A character set is the complete list of characters that a computer system can represent.

13. A binary code for the colour of each pixel is stored.

14. 300 bytes

15. Main memory is made up of storage locations, each of which has a unique address.

16. 128 addresses can be identified with 7 bit addresses.

17. Eight bits are required for 256 addresses.

18. The graphic contains 640 × 900 = 576,000 pixels.
    Each pixel requires 1 bit of storage.
    Total storage requirements = 576,000 bits = 576,000/8 bytes
    = 72,000 bytes.

19. The word size is 128 bits.

20. Storage = 1,600 × 288 bytes = 460,800 bytes = 460,800/1,024 Kilobytes
    = 450 Kb.

How did you do?

Answers correct

1–7 Not very good. You need to go back and learn this topic.

8–12 Reasonable. You know some of the work but look over pages 80–83 before moving on.

13–17 Good. You should move on but go back later and consolidate your knowledge.

18–20 Excellent. You have mastered this topic and can move on.

The syllabus and the exam

The syllabus

The syllabus for the exam consists of four main areas:

- Computer applications
- Communications and networks
- Commercial and industrial applications
- Computer systems

More details are given below.

Computer applications

General purpose packages
Word processing
Spreadsheets
Databases
Graphics
Desk top publishing
Presentation and multimedia
Web page creation
Expert systems

Communications and networks

Electronic communication
LANs and WANs
The internet

Commercial and industrial applications

Commercial data processing
Industrial applications/automated systems

Computer systems

Hardware
System software
Operating systems
Low level machines

Exam times

The amount of time given for each exam varies for every level. Computing Studies exam lengths are shown in the table below.

Level	Time
Credit	1 hour 45 min
General	1 hour 15 min
Foundation	1 hour

Be aware of the time during the exam and gauge your progress. If you are not halfway through the exam after half the time then speed up. On the other hand if you have completed half of the exam after fifteen minutes then you are almost certainly not writing enough detail into your answers and you should probably slow up and improve things.

Exam content and grades

The Credit, General and Foundation exams all consist of two components: knowledge and understanding and problem solving. The components are always allocated roughly the same amount of marks. You are given a grade for each of these components according to the table shown below.

Level	Percentage mark	Grade
Credit	70–100	1
Credit	50–69	2
General	70–100	3
General	50–69	4
Foundation	70–100	5
Foundation	50–69	6

The boundary for these grades can vary depending on the difficulty of the exam. For example 47% could be enough for a Credit 2 grade.

Overall grade

The overall grade for Standard Grade Computing is derived from three components. These are knowledge and understanding, problem solving and practical abilities. These are given the weighting **1:2:2**.

Practical grade

Your practical abilities grade is determined from practical work that is done in class. This grade is based upon coursework tasks that you have completed from non-programming, programming and project work. The grade that you achieve is not just determined from work that you have done at the computer but equally from the quality of your write-ups of the tasks. So take care to meet all of the requirements of the write-ups as outlined in the instruction sheets given to you by your teacher.

The worked example below will show you how the overall grade is calculated.

Component	Grade
Knowledge and understanding	2
Problem solving	4
Practical abilities	3

$(2 \times \mathbf{1} + 4 \times \mathbf{2} + 3 \times \mathbf{2}) / 5 = 16 / 5 = 3.2 =$
Overall Grade 3

The overall grade (3.2) is rounded to the nearest whole number (3).

Past papers

Actual past paper exams are a valuable resource to prepare you for the exam. These papers will give you a feel for the style of questions that are asked and how much emphasis is placed on the different areas of the syllabus. The past paper books also provide examiner-approved answers to give you a good idea of how much to write and how to word your answers.

Skills in answering questions

The front page of the exam

0860/407

NATIONAL TUESDAY, 1 MAY **ENGLISH**
QUALIFICATIONS 9.00 AM – 10.15 AM **STANDARD GRADE**
2007 Foundation, General
and Credit Levels
Writing

Read each question carefully.

Attempt **all** questions.

Write your answers in the space provided on the question paper.

Write as neatly as possible.

Answer in sentences wherever possible.

Before leaving the examination room you must give this book to the invigilator. If you do not, you may lose all the marks for this paper.

There is specific information on the front cover of the exam about how you are expected to answer the questions.

This is the information you will see.

Top Tip

In the exam there is no need to answer the questions in the order 1, 2, 3... You can consider starting at a question that you know well to help you relax before tackling the questions you find hard.

Take this information on board and know what is expected of you before the day of the exam.

Detailed answers

Marks are often lost for giving answers that are too short on explanation or do not give a reason to justify your answer.

The following question illustrates some common mistakes.

Question

Give two advantages of using a computerised database compared to using a manual database.

Answer 1

Quicker and neater.

Answer 2

Data can be accessed more quickly by selecting records according to criteria.

Data is stored on a hard disc which uses up far less space than paper records in filing cabinets.

Answer 1 shows that the student probably understands the advantages of a computerised database but has not answered in full sentences and has not given any reason.

Answer 2 gives two detailed reasons with a good justification of each advantage.

How much to write?

Each question will have a set number of marks allocated to it. In general try to make one point or give one reason for each mark. Use this as a general rule but feel free to give a fuller answer if you have time.

The text at the start of the question

Often there is a sentence or a paragraph at the start of a question to put the question in context or to give some information that is relevant to the question. This text at the start of the question has a bearing on your answer so make sure that you read it carefully.

For example, look at the question and answers shown below.

Question

A school keeps a database of students on the school role. Suggest why a record in THIS database may need to be amended.

Answer 1

Information needs to be updated.

Answer 2

A student may move house. Then the address field in his/her record will need to be updated.

Answer 1 is not specific enough and does not say why THIS database requires to be amended. So it is a poor answer.

Answer 2 is specific about why THIS database requires to be amended and gives an actual example about a student moving house. This is a good answer.

This might seem obvious but a lot of pupils lose marks by answering THEIR OWN questions and not the questions that are BEING ASKED.

Leaving time to read over your answers

It is usually a good idea to try and leave yourself time near the end of the exam to read over your answers. Ten minutes should be enough. In particular, the questions that involve calculations can guarantee you full marks **if your answer is correct** so check over your calculations. Answers that involve a description or explanation can also be checked to see if you have answered the question that is being asked and that you have given enough detail.

Questions

Question 1

An ice skating club sends out a personalised newsletter to all of its members once a month. Details of the members are stored on a database.

(a) Describe how the personalised letters can be created efficiently.

(b) The letter is stored in RTF format.

(i) What does RTF stand for?

(ii) What is the advantage of storing the letter in a standard file format such as RTF?

(iii) Name a standard file format used to store graphics files.

(3, 1, 1, 1)

Question 2

Sam South travels the world in his work for a model agency. He keeps a database of all his international flights.

Destination	Price (£)	Airline	Departure
Sydney	799	British Airways	Nov-27 2006
Rio	427	British Airways	May-03 2007
Hong Kong	379	British Airways	Nov-24 2007
Rio	377	British Airways	Feb-12 2007
Las Vagas	395	KLM	Dec-29 2006
Rio	389	KLM	Sept-11 2007
Sydney	910	Quantas	Dec-17 2006
Rio	479	Quantas	Oct-13 2007
Rio	339	Quantas	Dec-08 2007
New York	213	Quantas	Oct-26 2007
Paris	169	Quantas	Apr-21 2007

(a) How many fields are there in this database?

(b) What is the field type of each field?

(c) Sam wishes to obtain a printout of his flights to Rio which cost over £400. Describe how this could be done.

(d) A complex sort has been performed on the database on two fields. Describe the complex sort by naming the two fields and stating the order (ascending/descending) in which the fields have been sorted.

(e) Sam wants the price of the flights to be displayed in the records in Euros as well as in pounds. Describe how the database can be amended so that the prices are also displayed in Euros. (Use the conversion rate £1 = 1.5 Euros.)

(1, 4, 3, 4, 3)

Question 3

A flag has been created in a graphics package.

(a) Use a drawing of the flag (right) to illustrate each of the following editing operations:

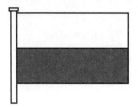

    (i) Rotate 180° clockwise   (ii) Crop

    (iii) Flip horizontally   (iv) Scale (enlarge)

(b) Explain the difference between high resolution and low resolution graphics.

(4, 2)

Question 4

A depute rector uses a spreadsheet to store the number of times students have received punishments in each of the first four weeks of term. Part of the spreadsheet is shown below:

	A	B	C	D	E	F	G
1	Name	Week 1	Week 2	Week 3	Week 4	Total	Detention
2	Monica White	0	0	2	0	2	NO
3	Sam Smith	1	3	0	4	8	YES
4	Wendy Wyper	2	0	0	0	2	NO
5	Peter Perfect	10	10	10	10	40	YES
6	Dwight Wyoming	5	2	0	0	7	YES

(a) It is required to add Winston Eagleburger to the spreadsheet but his name is too long to fit.

    What can be done so that his full name can be added to the spreadsheet?

(b) Cell F2 contains a formula to calculate the total for the first four weeks.

    Write down the formula that has been entered into cell F2.

(c) The formula in cell F2 has been replicated for the other students.

    Explain whether absolute or relative cell references have been used in the replication of the formula.

(d) Students who have received a total of more than six punishments are placed in detention.

    Cell G2 contains a function that automatically identifies students to be placed in detention.

    Part of the function is shown below. Copy and complete the function.

$$= \underline{\quad}(\underline{\quad}, \text{'Yes'}, \underline{\quad})$$

(e) Later on in the session the Depute Rector decides to monitor the students over a five-week period.

    How can the data for week five be added to the spreadsheet?

(1, 1, 2, 3, 2)

Question 5

Shown right is a diagram
of a client/server network.

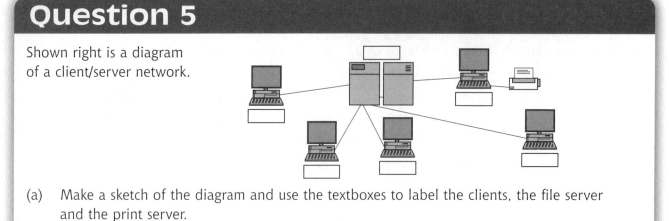

(a)   Make a sketch of the diagram and use the textboxes to label the clients, the file server
      and the print server.

(b)   Describe the function of the file server.

(3, 2)

Question 6

An employment office uses an expert system to suggest a suitable career for young people based
upon their interests and experience.

(a)   Which component of the expert system is used to enter the interests and experience of the
      young people?

(b)   Give an example of a rule or fact that would be stored in this expert system.

(1, 1)

Question 7

DTP and multimedia systems both include text and graphics.

(a)   Name two elements that appear in a multimedia system but not in DTP.

(b)   What is the difference between a multimedia presentation package and a multimedia
      authoring package?

(c)   What is the difference between animation and video?

(2, 2, 2)

Question 8

Winston Eagleburger works in the IT department of a Los Angeles company which hires out
stretch limousines.

(a)   Winston has just downloaded a software package from the internet which he thinks might
      be useful to the company accountants. The software is available for a trial period of
      one month.
      What name is given to software that is available for a trial period?

(b)   Winston uses the internet to look for a company that will clean the fleet of stretch
      limousines.
      Suggest how Winston could use the internet to perform the search.

(1, 2)

Question 9

There is an increasing use of robots in the manufacture of motor cars. One task performed by robots on the production line is the spraying of the car parts. These robots are fitted with **sensors** which provide **feedback** to the controlling computer.

(a)   Explain the meaning of the terms in bold.

(b)   The same robots are to be used to lift fragile glass pipes. The sensors are changed to pressure sensors to ensure the pipes are not crushed. Give two other changes that would have to be made to the robots.

(2, 2)

Question 10

At a point in a program the user is asked to enter the month in which he was born as a number from 1 to 12. The user enters 77 instead of 7 by mistake.

(a)   Name a process of error trapping that would find this error.

(b)   Explain why the program would not be able to find all the errors that occur when the month is entered and give a solution to this problem.

(1, 2)

Question 11

(a)   A database has 720 records. Each record stores an average of 320 characters. What is the storage requirement of the file in kilobytes?

(b)   Calculate the storage requirement for the black and white graphic shown right which has 3,500 x 1,870 pixels. (Give your answer in bytes.)

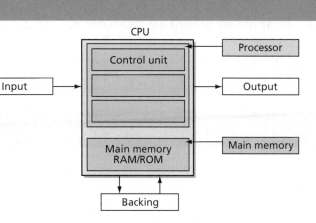

Question 12

A computer system is represented in the diagram right.

CPU

Processor

Control unit

Input

Output

Main memory RAM/ROM

Main memory

Backing

(a)   Name the two other components of the processor and describe their purpose.

(b)   A typical word size for current microcomputers would be 32 bits. Explain what is meant by a computer word.

(4,1)

Answers

Question 1

(a) 1 mark for each point.
- Create a standard letter in a word processing program.
- Use mail merge to insert names from a mailing list into positions in the standard letter.
- Obtain a printout of the personalised letters.

(b) 1 mark for each part.

   (i) Rich Text Format.

   (ii) A file in a standard format can be opened by other software packages.

   (iii) GIF or JPEG or TIFF or any other standard for graphics.

Question 2

(a) 1 mark.
Four fields.

(b) 4 x 1 mark for each field type.
Destination is a **text** field
Price (£) is a **numeric** field
Airline is a **text** field
Departure is a **date** field

(c) 1 mark for select or filter or similar term; 2 x 1 mark for specifying each field and condition to be met.
Select or filter the records where the Destination field = 'Rio'
AND the Price (£) field > 400.

(d) 2 x 1 mark for naming each field; 2 x 1 mark for stating ascending or descending for each field.
The database has been sorted on the Airline field in ascending order and the Price (£) field in descending order.

(e) 1 mark for inserting a field; 1 mark for stating that it is a calculation field; 1 mark for the formula.
Insert a calculation field called Euros which uses the formula = [Price(£)] *1.5.

Question 3

(a) 4 x 1 mark for each drawing of the flag showing the correct editing.
The cropping can be any part of the flag where the edges have been trimmed back.
The scaling can be any larger image of the whole flag.

Rotate 180° clockwise

Crop

(b) 1 mark for mentioning the size of the pixels; 1 mark for comparing the size of the pixels.
High resolution graphics are made up of a large number of small pixels.
Low resolution graphics are made up of a small number of large pixels.

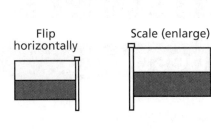

Flip horizontally   Scale (enlarge)

Question 4

(a) 1 mark.
The width of column A can be increased so that the long name fits into the cell.

(b) 1 mark.
The formula to be entered into cell F2 is **= B2 + C2 + D2 + E2**.

(c) 1 mark for stating that a relative cell reference has been used; 1 mark for an explanation of why a relative instead of an absolute cell reference.
A relative cell reference has been used so that when the formula is replicated the cell reference will change for each row.

(d) 1 mark for using an IF function; 1 mark for using the correct condition: F2 > 6;
1 mark for entering 'No' in the false part of the function.

= IF(F2>6,'Yes','No')

(e) 1 mark for insert a new column; 1 mark for change the formula for the total.
Insert a new column between columns E and F and edit the formula for the total to add up all five weeks.

Question 5

(a) 3 x 1 mark for each correct label.

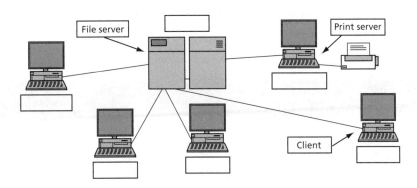

(b) 1 mark for stores files and programs; 1 mark for controls access.
The file server stores program and data files on the network and controls the access to files with the use of passwords.

Answers

Question 6

(a) 1 mark.
   Knowledge base.

(b) 1 mark.
   Any rule linking an interest to a job such as:
   IF FAVOURITE SUBJECT = 'Biology' THEN CAREER = 'Doctor'

Question 7

(a) 2 x 1 mark for each element.
   Multimedia systems have sound and video that do not appear in DTP.

(b) 1 mark for stand-alone package; 1 mark for can be programmed more.
   A multimedia authoring package has more extensive programming
   capabilities and can create a stand-alone package that can run without the
   program used to create it.

(c) 1 mark for description of frames in animation; 1 mark for real moving
   pictures in video.
   Animation is the creation of apparent movement by showing a sequence
   of still frames. Video is the movement of real pictures, usually captured by
   a digital camcorder.

Question 8

(a) 1 mark.
   Shareware.

(b) 1 mark for the use of a search engine.
   1 mark for giving suitable key words for the search.
   Winston could use a search engine and enter keywords such as:
   cleaners, Los Angeles, car.

Question 9

(a) 2 x 1 mark for each explanation.
   Sensors are devices that measure a quantity, such as motion, heat or light,
   and generate a signal that can be entered into a computer.
   Feedback is data that is sent back to a computer from a sensor.

(b) 1 mark for change the end effector; 1 mark for re-program the robot.
   The end effector or tool must be changed to a gripper and the program
   to control the robot will have to be changed.

Question 10

(a) 1 mark.
Validation.

(b) 1 mark for the explanation; 1 mark for verification.
The user could enter the wrong month, such as 3 or 12: these are still valid answers.
A solution is to verify the data: the same data is entered twice and any differences between the two versions can be found by the computer program.

Question 11

(a) 1 mark for understanding that each character requires 1 byte of storage;
1 mark for calculating the total requirement in kilobytes.
The storage requirement = 720 × 320 bytes = 230,200 bytes
= 230,400/1,024 Kb = 225 Kb.

(b) 1 mark for understanding that each pixel requires 1 bit of storage;
1 mark for calculating the total capacity in bytes.
The storage capacity = 3,500 × 1,870 bits = 6,545,000 bits
= 6,545,0008 bytes = 818,125 bytes.

Question 12

(a) 2 x 1 mark for identifying each; 2 x 1 mark for each description.
The ALU is the Arithmetic Logic Unit where calculations and logical decisions are made.
The registers are individual storage locations within the processor.
(b) 1 mark.
A word is a group of bits that is transferred as a unit within the CPU.

Glossary of terms

Absolute reference
A cell reference that does not change when it is replicated (filled down or across)

Accuracy
Correct and free from errors

Addressability
Main memory is made up of millions of storage locations, each of which is identified by a unique address.

Alignment
The way that text is lined up with the left-hand and right-hand margins of a page, e.g. left aligned, right aligned, centre aligned

ALU (Arithmetic Logic Unit)
A component of the processor that performs calculations and logical decisions such as AND and OR

Amending
The process of updating data to include changes

Analogue data
Data, such as temperature or pressure that changes continuously.

Animation
The illusion of movement created by showing a sequence of frames

ASCII (American Standard Code for Information Interchange)
A standard set of codes for representing characters in a computer system

Backing store
A device for permanent storage of data, such as a hard disc or a DVD

Backup
A copy of files on a storage device so that data can be recovered in the event of loss

Bar code
Parallel lines of varying thickness used to represent the code of an article

Batch processing
A processing mode where the data is collected and then entered into the computer in one go

Bit
A binary digit (1 or 0)

Broadband
A high speed internet connection that is always on

Browser
A program that displays web pages and can be used to surf the internet

Byte
A group of 8 bits

CAD (Computer Aided Design)
A program used by architects and engineers to create technical drawings

CAM (Computer Aided Manufacture)
The use of computers in all stages of the manufacturing process

CD-RW (Compact Disc Rewriteable)
An optical disc that can be read from and written to over and over again

CD-R (Compact Disc Recordable)
An optical disc that can be written to only once

CD-ROM (Compact Disc Read Only Memory)
An optical disc that can only be read from and never written to

Cell attributes
The format of the data in a cell, such as the number of decimal places or the way a date is displayed.

Cell formatting
The appearance of a cell, such as the cell width or fill colour

Cell protection
Locking a cell in a spreadsheet so that its contents cannot be accidentally or deliberately changed

CPU (Central Processing Unit)
The central part of the computer where programs are executed

Check digit
A digit attached to data to detect errors when the data has not been entered correctly

Client/server network
A computer network made up of servers, which provide a resource, and clients, that access the resources. Typical servers are file servers and print servers.

Glossary

Closed loop
A process control system which has feedback from sensors

Commercial software
Software that has to be paid for when it is downloaded

Compiler
A program which converts high-level language instructions into stand-alone machine code

Complex search
Using criteria to select records in a database by searching on two or more fields

Computed field
A field whose contents are calculated by a formula using the other fields in a record

Computer Misuse Act
Legislation that makes hacking and the sending of viruses illegal

Control language
A special purpose programming language used to control a machine

Computer engineer
A person who upgrades and repairs computer hardware

Control unit
A component of a processor that sends out signals to manage the fetching and execution of program instructions

Cropping
Trimming the horizontal and/or vertical edges of a graphic to display a part of the graphic.

Customising the HCI
Altering the HCI to suit an individual user

Data
Facts represented in a computer system in the form of numbers and characters

Data Protection Act
Legislation that protects the rights of individuals in society to privacy and security when their personal data is held on computer systems

Data subject
The person about whom data is held on a computer system

Data user
The person or organisation that uses the data held on a computer system

Degrees of freedom
The number of different ways in which a robot arm can move

Desktop publishing
A program that combines text and graphics to produce documents such as newsletters and pamphlets

Dial-up connection
A slow speed internet connection which has to be setup at the start of each session

Digital data
Data that changes in steps, such as the number of puppies in a litter

Direct/random access
Access to data stored on disc that can be read directly from any part of the disc

DVD (Digital Versatile Disc)
An optical disk with a high capacity. DVDs are used for storing multimedia data which requires a large amount of storage.

Dynamic link
When data is shared between two documents, changing the data in one document will automatically change the data in the other document.

EFTPOS (Electronic Funds Transfer at Point of Sale)
The transfer of money at the point of sale from a customer's bank account into a shop's bank account.

E-mail
The sending and receiving of electronic messages over a computer network

Embedded system
Hardware and software that performs a dedicated function as part of a larger system. For example, a microprocessor with software to operate a washing machine.

Encryption
Coding data so that it is scrambled and cannot be understood by people who gain unauthorised access

End effector
A tool, such as a paint spray gun or a ladle, installed at the end of a robot arm.

Expert system
A program that mimics the diagnosis or conclusions of a human expert in areas such as medicine or law

Fax
A device that sends and receives documents over the telephone line by coding them as binary numbers

Feedback
Data that is sent back to a computer from a sensor

Field
A category of data in a record

Field type
The data type of a file, such as numeric, text or date.

File
A named program or data document stored on a computer

File management
A component of the operating system that manages the files held on disc by keeping information in directories

File server
A computer on a client/server network that manages the storage of and access to files

Footer
A space at the bottom of each page in a document into which numbers, the date, text, etc, can be placed

Freeware
Software that is free and never has to paid for

Gigabyte (Gb)
1 Gb = 2^{30} bytes = 1,073,741,824 bytes

Hard copy
A printout of a document

Hardware
The physical parts of a computer such as the keyboard, floppy disc drive and processor chip, etc

HCI (Human Computer Interface)
The way in which the user communicates with a computer program

Header
A space at the top of each page in a document into which page numbers, the date, text, etc, can be placed

Hierarchical filing system
A filing system where a root directory contains sub-directories which themselves can contain further sub-directories and so on

High Level Language (HLL)
A programming language that uses everyday words in the instructions, for example Picture1.Print Volume.

Hotspot
An active area of the screen that triggers an event when the user places the mouse pointer over it

HTML (Hypertext Markup Language)
A language which describes the layout of the text, graphics, and other multimedia content of web pages.

Hyperlink
A link within a document or to another document that is usually activated by clicking on a piece of coloured text or a graphic

Inkjet printer
A printer that sprays droplets of ink through tiny nozzles onto paper to form an image

Integrated package
A software package consisting of two or more general purpose packages

Interactive processing
A processing mode that involves a dialogue between the user and the computer

Interface
A device which connects a peripheral to the CPU

Internet-ready computer
A computer that has the hardware and software already installed on it for instant connection to the internet

Interpreter
A program which converts high level language instructions into machine code one instruction at a time and executes them while a program is being run.

Keyboard shortcut
Using a combination of keys on the keyboard to choose an option in a program rather than using a mouse or a touchpad

Kilobyte (Kb)
1 Kb = 2^{10} bytes = 1,024 bytes.

Knowledge base
The component of an expert system that stores rules and facts about a problem

LAN (Local Area Network)
A computer network over a small site, such as a building or college campus, that uses cables or wireless connections

Laser printer
A printer that uses a laser to make an image on a photosensitive drum. The image is then transferred onto paper using a powder called toner.

LCD (Liquid Crystal Display)
A screen display that uses low power

Machine code
The computer's own programming language where instructions and data are written as binary numbers

MICR (Magnetic Ink Character Recognition)
Characters used at the bottom of cheques that are written in a special magnetic ink to help to prevent fraud

Mail merge
The process of inserting fields from a mailing list into places in a standard letter

Mainframe computer
A powerful and expensive computer used by organisations that need to process large volumes of data at speed

Megabyte (Mb)
$1 \text{ Mb} = 2^{20}$ bytes = 1,048,756 bytes

Memory management
A component of an operating system that manages the allocation of programs and data to areas of main memory

Mobile robot
A robot that moves around by using sensors under its base to follow a path. The path is formed by white lines painted on the floor or electric wires.

Modem
A device that converts digital data from a computer into a form that can be transmitted over telephone lines.

Multi-access
Two or more users can access one computer at the same time

Multimedia
An interactive computer system that displays text, graphics, video and sound data

Netiquette
A set of rules of good behaviour that should be followed when sending e-mails

Network
Two or more computers connected together so that they can share resources and communicate with each other

NIC (Network Interface Card)
A circuit board installed in a computer so that the computer can be connected to a network

Network manager
A person who manages the hardware and software on a computer network

OCR (Optical Character Recognition)
The identification of characters from their shapes to convert them into editable text

On-line
A term to describe a computer that is connected to the internet

On-line help
Assistance on how to perform a specific task provided within a program

On-line tutorial
A tour or lesson on the main features of a program provided within the program

Open loop
A process control system with no feedback from sensors

Operating system
A large program which manages the hardware and software of a computer system

Peripheral
A device connected to the CPU used for input, output or backing storage

Pixel
A picture element. The individual dots that make up an image are called pixels.

Printer driver
Software that allows a computer to communicate with a printer

Program
A set of instructions that a computer follows to solve a problem

Programmer
A person who writes, tests and maintains computer software

RAM (Random Access Memory)
A part of main memory whose contents can be read and written to by the processor

Real time
A processing mode where the data is entered and processed without any time delay. Used in booking systems etc.

Register
Registers are individual storage locations on the processor chip. They hold items of data that are required by the processor to perform its functions.

Relative reference
A cell reference that changes relative to its position when it is replicated (filled down or across)

ROM (Read Only Memory)
A part of main memory whose contents may be read but not written to by the processor

Replication
Copying a formula in a spreadsheet to other cells, such as filling down or filling across

Resolution
The size of the pixels in an image, usually described in dots per inch (dpi)

RTF (Rich Text Format)
A standard file format for text that stores some of the format such as **bold** and *italic*

Search and replace
Looking for a word or phrase in a document and automatically replacing it with another word or phrase

Sensor
A device that measures a quantity such as motion, heat or light and generates a signal that can be entered into a computer

Sequential access
Access to data stored on tape where other data must be read through in order to get to the required data

Shareware
Software that can be used for free, for a trial period after which it has to be paid for or deleted.

Smart card
A card the size of a credit card that has its own processor to store data

Software
The programs, such as the operating system, word processing and graphics that the computer can run.

Sorting
Arranging the records in a database into ascending or descending order

Standard file format
A file format that can be opened by a variety of software packages

Standard letter
A word processing document that can be used over and over again and can be personalised with fields from a mailing list using mail merge

Standard paragraph
A paragraph that has been entered once and then saved so that it can be used over and over again

Static link
When data is shared between two documents, changing the data in one document will not change the data in the other document

Stationary robot
A robot that is fixed to the ground and does not move around

Systems analyst
A person who manages the setting up of the hardware and software of computer systems.

Teleworking
Using computing technology and networks in order to work from home

Template
A document with some of the layout and structure already created. A template can be used as the basis for documents over and over again.

Terabyte (Tb)
1 Tb = 2^{40} bytes = 1,099,511,627,776 bytes

TFT (Thin Film Transistor)
A flat screen display that is made up of very small transistors

Transmission media
The communication channels used on a computer network

Validation
The process of rejecting data that is not sensible or valid and asking for it to be re-entered. For example, an age of 721 is not valid and the computer would ask for the age to be re-entered.

Verification
The process of checking data to see if it is accurate by entering the same data twice. The two versions are then compared and any discrepancies re-entered.

Video
Movement of real pictures which have usually been captured by a digital camcorder

Video conferencing
Communicating electronically with video and sound over a computer network

Virtual reality
Simulating the real world in a computer system that interacts with the user

Virus
A program which causes damage to a computer system and can replicate itself and spread to other computers.

WAN (Wide Area Network)
A computer network where the computers are linked by telecommunication channels over large distances. A WAN can link computers in different buildings on a street, between towns or even across countries.

WIMP (Window, Icon, Menu, Pointer)
A user-friendly HCI suitable for beginners that uses a mouse pointer to click on windows, icons and pull-down menus

Wizard
A dialogue between the user and the program guiding the user through a task

Word
A group of bits that is transferred around the processor as a unit

Wordwrap
If a word being keyed in at the end of a line becomes too long for the remaining space on the line, then it automatically comes down to the next line.

Index